Rebecca J. Craig

Once Upon a Nightmare

*Danica —
Stay strong & keep telling your own story.
Rebecca J. Craig*

THROUGH THE LOOKING GLASS
OF NARCISSISTIC ABUSE

All rights reserved. No part of this book may be used or reproduced, stored in a retrieval system, or transmitted in any form or by any means, electronic, mechanical, photocopying, recording, scanning, or otherwise, without written permission from the publisher except in the case of brief quotations embodied in critical articles and reviews. Permission for wider usage of this material can be obtained through Quoir by emailing permission@quoir.com.

Copyright © 2024 by Rebecca J. Craig

First Edition

Cover design by Matthew J. Distefano & Rafael Polendo (polendo.net)
Cover image by Rebecca J. Craig
Interior Layout by Matthew J. Distefano

ISBN 978-1-964252-00-1

Published by Quoir
Chico, California
www.quoir.com

Contents

Acknowledgements	VII
Introduction	IX
1. The Dream	1
2. Butterfly Effect	11
3. In God's Hands	29
4. The Compromise	39
5. In a Mirror Dimly	55
6. Sighs Too Deep for Words	69
7. Shattered	81
8. Puppet Master	91
9. Masquerade	105
10. Down the Rabbit Hole	115
11. Saving Grace	125
12. Moonlight Sonata	135
13. Vortex of Crazy	141
14. The Maelstrom	155

15.	Into the Wilderness	161
16.	Games with No Rules	171
17.	Bound	185
18.	Release	201
19.	Creation Song	211
20.	Renewal & Rebirth	217

For George

Acknowledgements

There are so many people to thank. Pr. Maryanne Kehlenbach, who encouraged me to write this memoir believing it would help others. Pr. Robyn Dee, who helped me hone my ideas as I kept going through the revisions. Pr. Rachel Ziese Hacker and Brittany Svoboda—two friends who never wavered, always told me the truth, and were there for me no matter what. My parents—I would not be the person I am without their love and support. For the members of my former congregation in Kearney, Nebraska that wrapped me in the love and the support I needed during one of the most difficult times in my life. There are too many of you to name individually, but you will forever hold a special place in my heart. Matthew J. Distefano for his patience and putting up with my random ideas during the publishing process. Keith Giles for having faith in my vision and story.

And for all the women out there who still feel trapped in their circumstances and for a variety of reasons cannot leave—know you are seen and not judged. And for all those who have had the courage to make hard choices for their own safety and sanity.

Introduction

My first year of seminary I took a class called "Telling the Story." It was a preaching course on how to preach the Biblical story. What I think I really learned is that when you embark upon the process of telling a faith story, you wind up also, at least in part, telling your own story. How you understand the piece of scripture you're about to turn into a ten-to-fifteen-minute sermon is determined by your own experiences and how you interpret the text based on those experiences. Yes, you spend time exegeting the text and understanding its historical and theological contexts, but ultimately, the power of the story lies in how you relate to it and how it speaks into your life. This is how it then speaks into the lives of others.

Your story thus becomes mingled with the Biblical story. The narratives take on new life as you apply them to your own life and situation. That in turn helps others to relate to these stories in ways they are able to connect them to their lives and experiences.

This is the power of story in general. Our stories are what bind us together. Our stories are how we relate to one another and share common human experiences. Storytelling helps us learn to empathize with others.

Scripture is not just the experience of humanity, but of humanity's experience of the divine. It's people across the millennia telling of their encounters with God and interpreting those encounters in light of their situations.

Storytelling is not limited to the written word, however. Art also tells a story. In fact, for the vast majority of human history, narrative art was used to tell the stories of people and civilizations. From the images carved in the caves of Lascaux, France, to the pictographs of ancient Egypt, to Renaissance cathedrals and basilicas—art has been the primary means for telling the narrative of a people. In fact, art many times overshadows what we read. Take, for instance, the story of Adam and Eve eating the fruit: how many people assume the text says they ate an apple? You have art to thank for that, even though apples were not indigenous to the ancient Near East. They originated in Kazakhstan, in central Asia, east of the Caspian Sea.

Or how many wise men attended the child Jesus? Art and music have both shaped our assumptions not only regarding how many attended, but when they arrived. Yet the text itself doesn't tell us how many there were, and it says they showed up to the house he was staying in, not the manger.

In addition to telling a story, art has the power to move people and evoke emotions that words can never do justice to.

As both an artist and a writer, it thus seemed fitting that the only way for me to ever really tell my own story was not simply in words, but through art as well. When I was in the deepest, darkest points in my life, words failed me. Art did not. It became the medium and mode of expression that I relied upon to express my emotions, to tell my story.

So it is with this book that I have combined both the artistic narrative of my journey with my writing. In fact, each chapter revolves around one of the pieces I created.

What you will find in this artwork is a strange mix of both faith and fairy tales. This may seem an odd juxtaposition of genres, but they really aren't.

Fairy tales are stories that many of us relate to. Fairy tales, like scripture, employ the use of allegories and symbols to convey deeper meanings. Characters and events often represent broader concepts or ideals.

The Disney versions of fairy tales tend to tap into our yearnings for the "happily ever after" ending where we find true love and ride off into the sunset. Those stories offer idealized outcomes to whatever situation we find ourselves in. We identify with Ariel because she doesn't fit in the underwater world she comes from and yearns to be part of another world (and not just for the sake of a boy). For those of us who are introverts, neurodivergent or LGBTQIA+, we relate to these yearnings and desires to "fit in" somewhere. On an even deeper level, while arguably nuanced, the 1989 version of the film deals with a layered critique of gender, sexuality, body dysmorphia, and even politics.

Mulan, made not quite a decade later, was similarly fighting against her country's tradition, the expectations of her family, and the mindsets of individuals who have had very specific and sexist ideas of what a woman's role is in the world.

In their original forms, however, most fairy tales take on darker themes and are typically cautionary tales with a moral point.

Ultimately, fairy tales help us to understand certain realities about our world, even though they tend to employ fantastical or even magical elements. One might say the same about scripture, which is no stranger to the miraculous and fantastical, known to even occasionally portray talking animals.

In many ways, both faith stories and fairy tales share many of these common themes.

However, many people would balk at the comparison, to suggest that the stories of sacred scripture could somehow be reduced to "mere fairy tales." I think that calling them "mere" fairy tales is an insult to the reality of how fairy tales are meant to operate as narratives in our lives.

It was again in seminary that I started making some of those connections. I remember asking an instructor one time "how do we respond when people say scripture isn't true, it's nothing more than a fairy tale?"

Her response was: "Whoever said fairy tales aren't true?"

This statement stuck with me, so much so that when I eventually became an instructor of World Religions at a local state college, I would ask my students on the first day of class: "Are fairy tales true?"

For the most part, I would get a resounding *"No!"* from everyone in the room.

I'd then challenge them to understand what truth was exactly.

Truth, you see, is not always found in historical facts.

Truth can be found in the much deeper meanings of metaphor and narrative stories that tell us deep truths about ourselves. Fairy tales, while not rooted in historical fact, are still commentaries on the societies that produced them.

Take the story of Hansel and Gretel, for instance.

Two children get lost in the woods, are captured by an evil witch in a gingerbread house and wind up killing the witch by throwing her in an oven and escaping. Now on the surface, the story seems ridiculous as there are clearly elements that cannot possibly be true, such as living in a gingerbread house.

However, beneath the fantastical façade lies a deeply symbolic truth as a commentary on German society.

The original story had the father and mother deliberately dropping their children off in the woods and abandoning them, addressing the very real fear at the core of most humans: being abandoned by someone they love.

At the time of the Grimms' penning of the tale, child abandonment due to extreme poverty had become quite commonplace.

Other symbols and themes resonate as well. Most notably the theme that runs throughout is one of transformation—as Hansel and Gretel at its core is a "rite of passage" type story.

At the start of the story, Gretel is seen as fearful and vulnerable, representing those aspects within ourselves; whereas Hansel is the clever, problem-solving one. When the witch finds them, it seems too good to be true—and of course it is. It is a reminder that nothing is really as it seems. All the fancy trappings we see many times harbor much darker realities.

The children are thus separated, and Gretel must learn to overcome her fears and dependence on Hansel. When the witch prepares to eat Hansel, Gretel is faced with a decision—whether to continue to obey the witch or stand up for herself and her brother. She chooses the latter and thus locks the witch in the oven and frees her brother.

On the way home, their roles have reversed. It is Gretel who is now confident and the one to solve problems having come into her own through her trials with the witch. Thus it is ultimately Gretel, by overcoming her fears and vulnerabilities, who helps them find their way home.

Facing difficulty and adversity is therefore the only way in which one transforms and grows.

Such themes and symbols run throughout most fairy tales. They are stories that tell deep truths about our lives.

Likewise, stories found within sacred scripture serve similar functions. They, too, are stories that address deep human truths and realities—whether they are historically factual or not.

Now I know in many faith circles, it's unthinkable to suggest that not every story in the Bible is rooted in historical fact. However, surely even those have to admit, a talking donkey seems more in the realm of fairy tale than historical reality.

In many ways, these stories and truths are far more meaningful when understood through their symbolic nature rather than their historical accuracy. The important element is how we relate to the story and what lessons it's trying to teach us.

After all, the theme of needing adversity and trials to grow up and transform can easily be seen in the sacred stories of, say, Adam and Eve.

Adam and Eve must face off with a representative of adversity, and thus set humanity on a path that is able to grow, change, transform and evolve through the challenges of no longer having every need tended to in the Garden of Eden. It explores the basic question of: are we more like God, or the rest of the animal kingdom we were created alongside? The Christian and Hebrew scriptures are about that transformation, not just with one another, but with humanity's relationship with God as well. This is hardly the only theme present within such stories, but definitely one of the themes.

The purpose of a fairy tale and a faith story serve different functions, however.

Fairy tales tend to be cautionary stories with a moral point.

Faith stories diverge from fairy tales on the issue of the divine. While they also are cautionary tales and typically have a moral point, faith stories are told to point us to a greater reality that exists beyond our own. They are written with the expressed purpose of creating faith so that we might actually be changed and transformed by the story. They are not mere cautionary tales. They seek to answer questions regarding our very existence and purpose. They exist to lay out a pattern of life for us.

Fairy tales carry no such divine purpose. While fairy tales are commentaries on our world, they are not typically seeking to tell us how we relate to the divine and the rest of creation. Thus, fairy tales are not even "myth," insofar as with mythos there is a belief system built around them, and they are used to explain the natural world.

Yet, both faith and fairy tales have been instrumental in how my art has taken form, and how I've expressed my own story. From an early career in story development at Disney Feature Animation to the pulpit, I've spent years reading the rich stories of scripture, folklore, fantasy and fairy tales. Whether I was reading them to turn them into an animated movie, to teach a class, or give a sermon, these realms have always crossed in my life.

Faith, because I needed my faith to sustain me during the worst moments. It was my faith community that supported me and lifted me up. It was the stories of scripture that gave me hope and that I clung to when in the depths of despair.

Fairy tales, because I'd spent my life dreaming of my "fairy tale" come true. That I'd one day find true love's kiss and meet my Prince Charming and live happily ever after with the white picket fence and two kids. Instead, I lived through a twisted Wonderland-like nightmare of shifting realities and abusive mind games. I found myself disillusioned by the Disney-fied versions of fairy tales when I found my own reality to be much more like the dark tales told by the Brothers Grimm.

Dating back as early as the first century, there were countless variations of fairy tales that conveyed moral, social, and/or political lessons through the narrations and characters, while also displaying the history of a culture. Namely, a culture that tended to be very violent toward women.

Thus, fairy tales tend to center around a woman who through intelligence, cunning or supernatural assistance (a fairy godmother or the like) manages to find her way out of some terrible situation.

I found myself identifying with these women.

There are any number of women throughout scripture as well who must use their intelligence and cunning to carve out their path in a culture that gave them few options. Stories of women who stood up against kings and tyrants, and without whom we would not have some of the Bible's most prominent characters such as Moses, David, and Jesus.

But women also endure countless atrocities against them. Hagar. Dinah. Tamar. The Levite's Concubine. Bathsheba.

What I've always found interesting about women in scripture is that scripture rarely blames women for their predicaments and actions. In fact, they are frequently rewarded for such things that we might question the ethics of: sleeping with one's father to produce offspring to save the world; pretending to be a prostitute to reclaim the few rights a woman had when those rights were abrogated; lying to protect one of the greatest prophets from Pharaoh's decree. They were simply trying to survive in a time and place where women had few rights and even fewer options.

Thus both fairy tales and faith stories tell us about how women survived the circumstances they found themselves in.

What neither the fairy tales nor the scriptures focus on, however, is the mental and emotional state of the women who find themselves trapped in these scenarios. Oh, the fear involved is conveyed clearly, but rarely do these tales focus on the depression, pain, and despair many women face when they're in the midst of such chaos and turmoil, feeling as though they have few to no options. The post-traumatic stress disorders that eventually develop.

Scripture, in particular, silences the voices of female victims. The two blatant rape victims, Dinah and Tamar, are never heard from again. Their stories become all about the men who do violent things in response. They have no voice.

Fairy tales, likewise, don't tell the tale of the wife who just decides to curl up and die. When she's reached the end of her rope and just feels she has no more options. Where getting out of bed is too hard to even contemplate. Curling up, distraught, trying to shut out the world as she turns in on herself, not wanting to have to face the world that swirls around her.

Such depression is a very real and typical side-effect not only of divorce, but abuse.

Both faith and fairy tales grapple with situations where abuse is prevalent. They are both commentaries on these injustices. They just don't tend to get into the nitty gritty realities of what it actually feels like to go through it.

The simply surviving from one moment to the next, day after day:

>Wake up.
>Breathe.
>Get up.
>Breathe.
>Get dressed.
>Breathe.
>Eat.
>Breathe.
>Walk out of the house.
>Breathe.
>Avoid getting hit by cars.
>Breathe.
>Arrive at work.
>Breathe.
>Do your job one minute, one hour, one day at a time.
>Breathe.
>Go home.
>Breathe.
>Eat.
>Breathe.
>Go to bed and try to sleep.
>Breathe.
>Repeat.

This book tells the tale of my quest to fulfill my fairy tale dreams that led me not into the "happily ever after" ending, but into the dark wilderness that resembled an upside-down realm of fantasy more than real life much of the time.

And of the faith that kept me going.

My art served as a medium for self-expression, conveying the depths of my pain, resilience, and faith. Drawing inspiration from both biblical stories and beloved fairy tales, the illustrations captured the essence of my emotions, mirroring my quest for healing and self-discovery.

It's a journey through a nightmarish Wonderland of chaos and confusion that I was dragged into—and how one can emerge on the other side. Several of my paintings incorporate the whimsy and wonder of Lewis Carrol's *Alice in Wonderland*, as in real life I was navigating a surreal and unfamiliar world, encountering unexpected twists along the way.

Ultimately, I'm writing this book because I want other women to understand they're not alone in this suffering. They're not crazy. What they're going through is not only hard, but devastating.

Again, I think back to the time fairy tales were originally written and the vulnerability of women. So many women are still vulnerable. So many are still trapped in their marriages or relationships because they do not possess the means or ability to leave.

Some have children and will be forever tied to their ex-husband and the craziness that goes along with their ex having a narcissistic personality disorder. Some will even be trapped, sadly, by their understanding of their faith.

I want them to know, God does not desire them to keep putting up with abuse. Any spiritual leader who tells you otherwise is also being spiritually abusive.

I want them to know not only are they not alone, but that there is hope. There is a light at the end of the tunnel. You do get through it.

And no, God has not abandoned you in the midst of it.

You just emerge very different than when you started.

When your dreams turn into nightmares, when your fairy tales turn into horror movies, you can come out the other end a survivor. You can live to tell the tale. You can eventually find wholeness and healing in your life.

God takes the shattered pieces of our lives and glues them back together into a new life, a new reality.

I also want to make it clear that while I talk a lot about the characteristics of narcissistic personality disorders, I am not a mental health counselor or therapist, nor am I trained in the discipline of mental health. I'm a pastor, not a therapist. (And despite what some pastors of other denominations may tell you, we are not qualified mental health practitioners, nor are we marriage counselors.)

Through my own therapy, study, and experiences, I have come to know and understand how people with narcissistic personality disorders behave. My ex-husband was diagnosed by a licensed mental health expert as having a narcissistic personality disorder, so my references to his disorder are not my own diagnosis or beliefs. My discussion about the disorder is based on the research I have done in the years since his diagnosis and then being able to recognize those behaviors in him and others like him. Still, that does not make me a licensed expert in the field and should not be taken as such.

I'm still on my own path to healing that has brought me to a place where I'm at least willing to see if happily ever after might be an option somewhere down the road. I pull no punches: I made a ton of mistakes, and as I wrote this book, I seriously wanted to shake my past self and just go "what is wrong with you?!" Honestly, I want to shake my present self much of the time when I see myself repeating the same mistakes and behaviors. I trust too easily; forgive too readily. I don't listen to my internal voice that tells me to break it off or run because, somewhere, I always have this fear of ending up alone.

As much as I say alone is better than trapped in a bad situation, after years of loneliness, one forgets how bad it can be when you're with the wrong person.

That history and those patterns are what led me to my horrible situation. Chasing a fairy tale dream is how an otherwise intelligent woman found herself married to a narcissist.

I hope the art I created during that time period speaks to you and conveys the emotional realities that so many faith stories and fairy tales tend to leave out.

ONCE UPON A NIGHTMARE

So I'm going to tell you my tale, such that it is. I'm sorry if my story resonates, but not sorry if it helps you feel less alone. I hope this offers a unique perspective on the intersection of faith, fairy tales, and the transformative healing power of art in your own life.

One
The Dream

"It can take years to mold a dream. It takes only a fraction of a second for it to be shattered."

— Mary E. Pearson, *The Kiss of Deception*

ONCE UPON A TIME there was a woman who seemed to have everything in the world going for her. At the age of twenty-four she was working her dream job in Hollywood in the story development department of Disney Feature Animation. She hob-knobbed with celebrities, sat in on meetings with the late Steve Jobs, pitched ideas to Michael Eisner, and talked daily on the phone joking with Elton John's husband, David Furnish, like they were long-lost friends. She was invited to special concerts with Phil Collins, and even spent two weeks sitting outside Sting's temporary office on the third floor of the animation building.

Most people spend at least half their careers and countless years trying to achieve that kind of position. I'd done it in a year and a half after moving to Burbank from Nebraska, starting out with no job, no money, and no connections. Yet here I was eighteen months later living the dream. It was only going to get better from here, right? Next stop, Producer or Vice President of Creative Development! Maybe owning my own production company? The sky was the limit! Once someone gets their foot in the door in Hollywood, you're in. You have it made.

Right?

Seventeen years later, I was a pastor living in a small town in south central Nebraska, trying to navigate the upside-down world of the federal penal system and trying to escape the web of deceit and lies I'd been pulled into by my malignant narcissist husband.

Cue the record player scratching to a halt.

Wait. I'm sorry, what? How did that happen exactly?

Well...there was one small problem with living the Hollywood dream.

It was never the dream I really wanted.

I know, I know, it sounds crazy, because being a parish pastor in small town Nebraska wasn't exactly my dream, either. In fact, that was probably the farthest thing from a dream I ever had growing up. I didn't grow up particularly "religious" aside from I had my own beliefs, went to church sporadically as a kid, but pretty much didn't darken the doors of a church between the ages of eighteen and twenty-eight. I found the Bible and other religious topics fascinating, but certainly never saw it as a career path.

No, my dreams were much more ordinary.

Starting at the age of two, I had a very simple dream: to get married and raise a family. Maybe not popular in today's world when a girl can grow up and become...well apparently not President of the United States (not yet anyway) but at least Vice President. Or, you know, maybe a Hollywood Studio Executive.

Anyway, at the age of two, I informed my parents that I was going to have a little boy and a little girl just like they had—but first, I had to "find me a man." Setting aside the whole improbability of my being able to control the gender of my future unborn children, the fact that I comprehended the simple reality that I "needed a man" to achieve this outcome seemed rather astute in hindsight for a two-year-old.

That was the dream. I wanted the fairy tale. I wanted the Disney-esque, meet your Prince Charming, fall in love and live happily ever after type of story for my life. It worked for my parents, why not for me? My physician father and med-tech mother met at a bar in Omaha when my dad was in medical school. She was dressed like a pumpkin in an orange and brown-trimmed outfit (it was the sixties, come on), asked my dad if he had a cigarette, then proceeded to ask if he was married. The rest, as they say, is history. Over fifty years later, they're still happily married and living the life I always dreamed for myself.

Like I said—nothing strange or unusual in my dream. Disney movies wouldn't be so popular if they didn't tap into those underlying desires so many of us already have.

Have you ever read actual fairy tales, though? Not the Disney-fied versions we took a lot of creative license with, but the originals by Hans Christian Anderson, the Brothers Grimm or Charles Perrault? While some of them might end with the words "and they all lived happily ever after," more often than not, that's not actually how they unfold.

Take the *Little Mermaid*, for instance. The original story involves the mermaid making a deal with the sea witch whereby she can only come on land to be with the handsome prince if she drinks a potion that makes it feel like she is walking on knives at all times. Now in post-Disney fairy tale world, you would expect her selfless act to end with the two of them getting married.

Nope. The prince marries a different woman, and the Little Mermaid's deal with the witch means she must die. The big catch? Mermaids don't have souls like humans. So the sea witch gives her one more opportunity to live: kill the man she loves.

Instead, unable to kill him as he sleeps next to the other woman, the mermaid takes her own life and her body dissolves into sea foam, as she turns into a luminous and ethereal earthbound spirit. For the next three hundred years she is given the opportunity to do good deeds and ascend to heaven, thus earning a soul.

While this is a story about eternal rewards for selfless sacrifice in the end, it certainly isn't what most of us would consider a "happy ending," in the most traditional sense of the meaning. Love did not win out. Happily ever after with the man of the girl's dreams didn't transpire. There was no riding off into the sunset on a boat together.

Or consider the original 1634 Italian version of *Sleeping Beauty*, where the princess is raped in her sleep (the King who runs across her and thinks she's dead naturally decides to have sex with her dead corpse. Which, ew?) and awakened not by the kiss of her true love, but by her newborn twins that she was impregnated with by her rapist. When her baby-daddy, the King, brings them to the palace, his wife tries to kill them (that's right, he's married to someone else). That's eventually thwarted, and the princess marries her rapist. (Thankfully Charles Perrault and the Brothers' Grimm both ditched the rape scene in their versions of the story.)

Or what about *Snow White*? The wicked queen in the original German version is made to dance wearing a pair of red-hot iron shoes until she falls over dead.

These are not happy stories. They are not what we think of when we say we "want the fairy tale."

These were definitely not the types of fairy tales I meant when I wanted to live the fairy tale. I suppose I find it rather ironic that I even wound up working for Disney Animation. I wanted to tell the fairy tale stories I hoped my own life would end up like. Mulan—the girl who went searching for who she truly was and still somehow ended up with the handsome Shang in the end. Beauty and the Beast—the beast turns into the handsome prince she's loved all along. Lucky girl. Tarzan—Jane winds up with her handsome jungle man.

We want the happy ending.

We don't want throwing ourselves into the depths of the sea as the man we love marries another woman.

We want the prince who delivers us from our slumber with true love's kiss—not a rapist who takes advantage of us while we're unconscious.

Yet reality sadly mirrors the original tales far more closely than "happily ever after." Most fairy tales and folktales are rooted in some sort of social commentary. They weren't originally meant to be told to little girls who just wanted to dress like her favorite princess.

Charles Perrault said that the lesson of his version of *Sleeping Beauty* was: be patient waiting for love.

Be patient? Well, my dream of true love would elude me for the first thirty-eight years of my life. How patient does one need to be exactly? It was filled with many frogs, and as a result, I found myself eventually chasing after other dreams in an attempt to fill the void of the unfulfilled fairy tale. It was this drive and this desire to fulfill my childhood fairy tale dream that likely led me to eventually marry not my Prince Charming, but his evil twin with a narcissistic personality disorder. By the time I met him, I felt the need to set aside my standards of what I was ideally looking for. I realized I didn't necessarily need Prince Charming, just Prince Good-Enough.

Word to the wise: do not compromise your standards. Ever. Prince Good-Enough will more often than not turn into the villain rather than the savior figure in your life. I guess I should have paid more attention to the moral of Perrault's version of the *Sleeping Beauty* story.

Now, part of the issue was I never saw myself as an attractive teenager. I was awkward, slightly overweight until I was about seventeen, and like many a Disney princess, I just didn't fit in anywhere. Then I discovered the fun world of eating disorders and near-anorexic starvation diets that dropped me down to a mere one hundred ten pounds my senior year of high school in an attempt to fit whatever standard of beauty I thought boys were looking for. I didn't date and boys had expressed very little, if any, interest in me.

After all, I'd had a crush on the same boy since the seventh grade. It was a small enough school in rural Nebraska that I can't say he didn't know I existed—he knew who I was. He just didn't care. There was no *Sixteen Candles* awkward girl who manages to grab the attention of the hunky senior who casts aside the prom queen because he finds you "interesting." John Hughes films were modern day fairy tales...and a load of crap, by the way.

The near-anorexic diet seemed to work to some degree outside the realm of my own high school. At least in my own mind, my first real love that seemed to be reciprocated in some capacity occurred while I was at Space Camp's Aviation Challenge in Huntsville, Alabama of all places. My father, while a doctor, had also been a private pilot and owned a small single-engine plane. I enjoyed being his co-pilot upon occasion. While it wasn't anything I intended to pursue as a career, it sounded like fun and was of interest to me. Likely because it was one of the few things I felt I could bond with my father over since I didn't like hunting or fishing.

My first love was a skinny but gregarious sixteen-year-old boy I met my first day as we stood in line to pick up some sort of important information or article of clothing. Probably our squadron t-shirts. I honestly don't remember.

What I do remember was he saw me wearing my Depeche Mode t-shirt from the concert I'd gone to at the Red Rocks in Denver earlier that summer, and commented on it. We struck up a conversation regarding our favorite techno-industrial band. It was like we were bonded at the hip for the rest of the week. By the time we left, we were promising to write and call each other, and he even left me a note telling me how much he wished I lived in his state rather than Nebraska so we could be together.

Be still my romantic teenage heart.

We called each other weekly, wrote each other long, ridiculous letters going on and on about the mundane details of our teenage lives. I went to see him over New Year's, and he came down to take me to my prom.

What I failed to recognize was that while I had no prospects on the horizon, he had a girlfriend that he just never really made clear was his girlfriend. Still, it had become clear by May of 1991 that the distance had taken its toll on whatever romantic notions I may have had in my head about him being my Prince Charming, and we parted ways without much fanfare. Still, my freshman year of college he called me up because he was passing through town on his way to Breckenridge to go snowboarding. We still talked on the phone occasionally, wrote a letter here and there. We'd see each other again my senior year of college on a return trip from his annual visit to Colorado. There was still some sort of undefined bond there that neither one of us seemed to know what to do with.

In the meantime, my second semester of college I met and began dating my first and what would turn out to be my only boyfriend of my entire college career, which was really quite sad given the actual relationship only lasted about two months before I caught him cheating on me. The rest of my college career would be just him popping in and out of my life.

I will confess that his freshman roommate was literally the "one who got away." I was still pining over the jerk who cheated on me when his roommate made it clear he was interested in me. I just didn't "feel that way" about him and kept him firmly in the "friend zone" for the next two years. It wasn't until he moved to Cheyenne, Wyoming, to go to aviation mechanics school that I realized I'd been a total idiot. I called him up one day to tell him I'd finally come to my senses. I had a whole scenario worked out in my head of how amazing this was going to be.

"Hey! I've got great news! I was just planning on calling you!" he said when he answered the phone.

"Oh?" I asked absently, not really wanting to hear his good news because I was so giddy about my own. Still, I paused and waited to hear what great thing was going on his life that he couldn't wait to tell me.

"I just got engaged! Now why were you calling?"

I want to say I made that exchange up, but nope. That's how it went. Literally. What's worse is after I met his fiancé when they moved back to Lincoln a few months later, I really liked her, too. They're still happily married almost thirty years later. If there's one regret I have in this life, it's that I didn't pull my head out of my butt faster on that one.

Shortly after I graduated with my degree in Broadcast Journalism in December of 1995, I received a letter from my first love who was now attending helicopter school down in Florida. I don't remember much of what that letter said except that at one point he made the statement, "I believe we are soulmates."

Well. Here I was, freshly graduated from college, in a job I didn't care for in the least as I was hired straight out of the broadcast journalism program at the University of Nebraska to make training videos for a cable test equipment company, when I get a letter from the boy I'd pretty much been in love with since I was seventeen. It was five years later, and here he was calling me, after all this time and distance, his soul mate.

My fairy tale come true. At last. He really *was* my Prince Charming!

What did I do? What any girl does when she's chasing her childhood dream and the man of those dreams tells her he thinks they're soulmates: I hopped on a plane to Florida with notions of happily ever after. I figured if things went well, I could begin looking for a broadcasting job. Surely a local news station would have need of a young college graduate, right?

Well, that dream was quickly shattered a few days into my visit when his new seventeen-year-old girlfriend (you read that right, but it was technically legal) showed up on his doorstep and demanded he make a choice between her and me.

He chose her.

I guess soulmates don't stand up against skinny little seventeen-year-old blond sex-pots with pixie haircuts.

I was utterly devastated. Not only had I lost the dream, but I'd lost someone who had been an important part of my life. I don't know what kind of relationship I would have characterized ours as prior to that moment—it wasn't strictly friends nor was it fully romantic. Whatever it was, it didn't deserve to be dragged through that kind of garbage.

I changed my departing flight and left the next day and spent the night at his cousin's place. In order to go see him, I'd taken the cheapest flight I could find—I was a recent college graduate after all earning a whopping seventeen grand a year—so I'd taken a flight out of Kansas City which was three hours from Lincoln where I lived. When I went to pick up my car, I discovered it had a flat tire.

So. There I was. Heartbroken and stranded in a strange city, trying to change a tire in the parking garage of the Kansas City airport late at night.

Much to the dismay of my parents, I made a decision as I was driving back that night to pursue a different kind of dream. College had been a bust in terms of finding Prince Charming. I needed a new start. I needed a different dream.

My new dream wasn't as strong as the one I'd had since I was two years old, but I did have a Plan B in case Prince Charming never found his way to me.

I could focus on my career instead. I loved writing. While I had a degree in broadcasting, I had zero desire to actually do the news at this juncture.

It was one thing to imagine yourself winning a Pulitzer Prize for some hard-hitting investigative news segment. It was another to realize that sensationalism was rapidly becoming the future of what would become known as info-tainment. The rise of Fox News and their over-the-top style of sensationalizing the news stories of the day was quickly beginning to bleed into other realms of the industry. Other twenty-four-hour news outlets as well as networks were beginning to follow the same model.

I decided I wanted nothing to do with that and determined if I was going to entertain people for a living, I might as well just write my own imaginative stories where the audience at least knew that my work was fiction. Plus, I was an introvert, and let's just say hounding people for an interview wasn't really my style.

Trading in my notions of a Pulitzer Prize for an Academy Award became the new dream I adopted for myself.

And maybe, just maybe, moving from a city of a quarter of a million people, to the second largest city in the United States with a metropolitan population of over twelve million, I might have better odds of finding my elusive Prince.

Two
Butterfly Effect

"Small shifts in your thinking, and small changes in your energy, can lead to massive alterations of your end result."

— Kevin Michel,
Moving Through Parallel Worlds To Achieve Your Dreams

IT WOULD BE A series of choices and events that would lead me from Hollywood to the ministry. My own "butterfly effect" of choices and experiences that would send me down this strange trail.

In Disney's *Beauty and the Beast*, Belle asks Gaston, "What do you know about my dreams?" when he tries to tell her what she should want out of life. I appreciated and even envied some of Belle's independence and desire for more than a provincial life. I struggled because on the one hand, I'd have been fine with the provincial life, yet that didn't seem to be what was going to happen for me. If the provincial life was not an option, then surely embarking on an adventure that would take me to a great wide somewhere would have to suffice. And maybe, like Belle, in pursuit of that great adventure, I'd stumble upon my own Prince hidden among all the beasts.

In April of 1996, my U-haul was packed, and my mother was sobbing—firmly convinced that twenty-three-year-old recent journalism graduates who moved to California with no job and no money would wind up doing one of two things: prostitution or porno flicks. Or both.

I had a lot of incentive to prove my mother wrong on this front. My father had offered me a thousand dollars to not move, and let's just say was so angry when I rebuffed that offer that he refused to speak to me for three months after I left.

To be fair, my departure was perhaps not undertaken the best way. My parents had just spent a month in Australia, and while they were gone, I'd made all the plans to move. I'd spent countless hours at my second job, bartending at a local Comfort Inn and Suites, planning my move with the father of my best friend from high school, who used to come into the bar for a beer and we'd play backgammon together.

My leaving three days after my parents returned home wasn't the kindest way to go about leaving. The problem was, I knew if they were given enough of an opportunity to talk me out of it, I would have never left. I knew I had to keep my resolve, and this seemed the best possible way to do that, even if it was traumatic for my parents.

Armed with my single screenplay and a plethora of short stories I'd written during college, I arrived in Burbank with no job, no friends, a drained bank account and a credit card bill that I'd used to cover my remaining moving expenses. I wasn't all that different from thousands of other young, bright-eyed college graduates from the Midwest who thought they were going to move to Hollywood and eventually wind up on stage one day saying, "I'd like to thank the Academy…"

Okay, maybe my ambitions were somewhat less grandiose. I would have been perfectly happy being a regular old screenwriter who didn't have to stand on Sunset Boulevard hoping the ending to *Pretty Woman* was actually a thing and confirming my mother's worst fears.

It wasn't easy. In fact, my first year was pretty rough. I initially worked as a receptionist in a temp agency, sending other people out on jobs that I wanted to be going on myself. But I didn't have the computer skills necessary to actually go out on most temp assignments. I didn't know Microsoft Word or Excel. Remember, this was 1996. Windows 95 had just come out, and my personal computer was some generic 286 kilobyte monochrome screened dinosaur that ran DOS and WordPerfect. It couldn't even run the early dial-up versions of AOL.

So in my free time, I used the computers at the temp agency to teach myself these programs. About a month or so later, I went to a different temp agency and aced their tests. They immediately sent me to Disney Interactive to play video games for ten dollars an hour—three dollars an hour more than what I'd been making as a receptionist.

For the record, that did not require I know Word or Excel.

I also had no idea what I was doing. My first day I sat and glanced over at the other testers to see how they were able to get the game started. Windows 95 was completely foreign to me. That hadn't been part of the testing process for the temp agency.

I at least knew that the CD-ROM wasn't a cup holder.

By looking over the shoulders of others, I managed to get the game up and running so I could start testing for bugs, crashes, compatibility, and language accuracy.

How on earth was playing video games rough, you might ask? Try spending three months straight on the *Lion King Activity Center* listening to Rafiki speak in Korean, Italian, German, Dutch, Spanish and French and tell me you're not ready to jump out a window and test the laws of gravity, too.

Especially since I didn't speak any of the aforementioned languages, with the exception of some Spanish.

I eventually moved on to bigger and better things—which meant being transferred off the night shift onto the day shift and working on the domestic products that were in English: the *Toy Story Activity Center*, and the *Toy Story Storybook*. By my third month there, I was the assistant lead tester on the *101 Dalmatians Animated Storybook*—my one claim to fame. My name even wound up in the credits on that last one. Not that thirty years later anyone owns any of these games anymore.

Still, testing video games for a living wasn't exactly the reason I'd moved halfway across the country and broken my mother's heart. Don't get me wrong, I met and worked with a lot of really awesome people. People who were former child actors, like Matthew Laborteaux, (you probably know him better as Albert Ingalls from Little House on the Prairie), people who would go on to be on shows later in life like *Dexter*, be part of the Academy Award winning voice-over cast of *Coco*, and a lot of people who had been struggling for up to a decade to just get their big break in the writing world. Or there was the party I got to attend at Bella Lugosi's home because I worked with Tim Lugosi, his grandson. I had the distinct, um, honor(?) of meeting the guy who played "Chainsaw" in *Summer School* with Matthew Laborteaux's brother, Patrick Laborteaux of *J.A.G.*: the closest connection I ever had to Mark Harmon. *(*Swoon.*)* Plus a whole slew of other people you've never heard of that were amazing.

Call it fate, divine intervention—whatever you will—but eleven months later the department went through a slow period, and several of the testers like me wound up without work for a week or so. The thing about temping is you have no benefits—no vacation pay, nothing like that. A week without work in the Los Angeles area when you lived from paycheck to paycheck and typically worked overtime and double time just to make ends meet meant you didn't get to slack off. Not even for a week.

So it was back to the temp agency and being sent out on various jobs. My next assignment: a week filling in for the secretary in the President and Vice-President of Disneyland International's office.

It would be a week that would change my life.

Apparently, the trick to moving your career forward is to not be a temp that just sits and reads a book. I had this bizarre notion that when I was sent to do a job, I was supposed to do the job. Call it my Midwestern work ethic. It impressed the vice president that not only did I arrive on my first day sans the book, I attempted to stumble my way through my first-ever expense report. Those Excel skills I taught myself were finally of some use. At the end of the week, he said he wanted to hire me. He didn't have any open positions in his department, but he'd like to help me. What did I want to do?

"I want to work in story development for Disney Feature Animation!" I blurted out.

Where did that come from? Well, it wasn't so strange if you thought about it. I loved art. I had taken art in high school and graduated from college only three credits shy of both art and art history minors. It was my hobby. And therapy.

While I'd been working at Disney Interactive, friends had not only built me a computer, but given me programs like Photoshop to work on after I'd been playing with a program at work called *Disney's Magic Artist*. I'd created a whole story book with the program about Simba and Nala from the *Lion King* running off to Vegas where Simba became a pimp and Nala a Vegas showgirl. I wish I still had a copy of that but, alas, it's been lost in all the moves over the decades since.

My friends convinced me I had a knack for this art and story-telling thing, and I had begun to gain a new appreciation for the animation medium.

Oh, and—I loved fairy tales. My bookshelves to this day are filled with various renditions of fairy tales and children's books.

So when asked "what do you want to do," working in animation sprang immediately to my lips. After all, when my mother had come to visit me about three months after I moved, just to make sure I really wasn't a prostitute or porn star, I'd pointed at the ship-shaped building along Riverside Drive in Burbank with the Sorcerer's hat that was the Disney Animation headquarters and informed my mother: "One day, I'm going to work there."

As luck would have it—the Vice President of Disneyland International was good friends with the Vice President of Human Resources at Disney Feature Animation. He picked up the phone and gave her my name.

Six months later, after a brief stint working for an organization called Women in Film, I was walking into the Animation building on Riverside Drive at the Disney Studios as a full-fledged employee working in the Story Development department.

My new dream was becoming a reality. I got to work on some pretty great films: *Mulan, Tarzan, Toy Story 2, Lilo and Stitch, Treasure Planet,* and *Emperor's New Groove,* just to name a few. I wasn't necessarily living the fairy tale, but I at least was making fairy tales for others.

Now, I know several people think the most interesting part of any memoir I would write would be who I met and worked with in Hollywood. Reality is, it was a job like any other. Yes, I met a lot of stars. Tom Hanks, Tim Allen, Sting, Phil Collins, Steve Jobs, Tim Conway, Phil Hartman, Steve Martin, Bette Midler, David Spade, John Goodman, and as previously mentioned, I talked almost daily with Elton John's husband, David Furnish.

The thing is, though, they were not people who impacted my life. They were people I met in passing. They were hands I shook and occasionally mouths I would feed when I ordered food for a meeting. (Trying to deal with Steve Jobs' strictly vegan diet was always a challenge when ordering food for an entire room of executives.) People who, if I were to meet them again today, would have no clue who I was or that I ever existed in their orbits.

Funny thing about dreams, though. They change over time. Reality has a tendency to rip off the shiny veneer and force you to really evaluate what you want in life.

For three years, I watched the lives of the successful Disney executives I worked with on a daily basis. In particular, I watched my direct supervisor, a single woman in her mid-thirties who was the Vice President of Creative Development. She went to premieres and a slew of other Hollywood events. Always with her best friend, a gay man, on her arm.

I began asking myself: is that going to be my life as well? I mean, I hadn't *totally* given up on my lifelong dream, had I? After all, there were twelve million people in the Los Angeles metro area. Surely I could find *one* of them to date? I had plenty of LGBTQIA+ friends around me that I could take to events like my vice president did, and I loved them dearly. It just wasn't the same. (Though they frequently would remind me that if I'd switch sides, they had plenty of lesbian women they could hook me up with. As appealing as that may have sounded, I also knew myself well enough to know that I was most definitely straight.)

Thus far, my only venture into the dating realm had been a guy I'd met and worked with at Disney Interactive. That fell apart shortly after I began working for Animation. Not because I'd started working in Animation, but because we had a lot of very different cultural views. He was Persian, and his family had moved here from Iran seventeen years earlier to escape the coup that ousted the Shah. After a year and a half of dating, it soon became clear that I did not fit well into his larger family dynamic, and that created a rift.

He'd gotten angry at me because I didn't talk a lot during Thanksgiving dinner and his mother thought I was being rude. I wasn't being rude intentionally. They spoke Farsi the whole time, and I didn't. I literally had no idea what the conversation was even about, thus it was difficult to add anything. When he demanded that I apologize to his mother for not engaging in a conversation that I couldn't even understand, that pretty much ended the relationship.

Also, there's a reality to working in Hollywood. You don't succeed just by simply "doing your job" really well. You have to play the game. You have to scheme and take advantage and at times backstab others in order to secure your own advancement. Or, in many cases, deal with the Harvey Weinsteins of the industry.

Now, working in Animation, the latter was not really an option as every single one of my male supervisors was gay. I couldn't Harvey Weinstein my way into a better job. (Not that I would have or would have wanted to. Just pointing out that the option wasn't even available to me.)

However, backstabbing opportunities for securing my advancement *were* available to me. When a story editor position became available, I wanted to throw my hat in the ring for the job. I felt all the work I'd been doing providing coverage on books and scripts for the current story editor would make me a shoo-in for the position.

Then, when I sat down with some of my superiors and expressed my interest, I was told that despite having busted my keister for the past three years, they had decided that the other development assistant they had hired at the same time as me was going to be the one they groomed for promotion when the time came. It was a decision they'd made upon hiring us both three years earlier.

I was never even in consideration for the position.

Also, the fact that when my direct supervisor had been promoted to vice president of the department and I'd opted to stay her assistant and take a pretty significant pay raise, I'd forfeited the right to be promoted to the story editor position. Literally no one explained to me when they asked if I wanted to keep being my supervisor's assistant that I'd be sacrificing any hope of ever advancing beyond that role.

Yes, I was angry. Doubly so because the individual they gave the promotion to had been someone whose constant ineptness I had covered for. I knew he would fail miserably at this new position. A part of me thought "fine, just wait it out. Stop helping him and let him fall flat on his face and then take over his position after you prove you could do it better."

Oh, I had a plan in place. It wasn't overly underhanded, just sort of a sit back and let the guy fail approach. Still, when I got up in the mornings, I would look in the mirror and hate myself. Because that wasn't who I was.

I loved my job. I loved doing what I did. Sitting back and letting someone else fail meant everyone failed at some level, and I hated that idea.

Ultimately, I decided that was not the person I wanted to be. So instead, I quit. I walked away and began working in real estate marketing and advertising.

Do I regret that decision? In some ways, yes. I definitely miss the creative environment I was immersed in. I truly enjoyed the process of taking a film from concept, to outline, to script, to production. In Story Development, we walked all the way through the life of a project, from the moment it was conceived and pitched, to the moment it wound up in theaters across the country. (Ironically, at Disney, the Story Development people who conceive of the idea and help turn it into a reality are never included in the end credits. That was always wild to me. So no, you'll never see my name at the end of a Disney Animated film. The lawyer's assistant got their name in credits, but not the Story Development people.)

I loved walking into my workspace every day and seeing the beautiful concept art and storyboards the artists would hang along the walls of the third floor where I worked. I'd purposely take the spiral staircase in the hat section of the building every morning instead of the elevators so I could see what was happening on the production floors below us. It was always fun to also walk by the office that was located in the Sorcerer's hat, which at the time was occupied by Walt Disney's nephew, Roy O. Disney.

Leaving all that behind was not an easy decision, and one I was grieved over. Still, I knew the environment had changed. I had other people from other departments constantly coming up to me asking me why I didn't apply for the Story Editor position. They'd grow angry when I explained that I had and the reason why I was not being considered. I grew tired of the anger and resentment coming from both me and others that I worked with. Even at that relatively young age I realized this would become very toxic very quickly. I didn't want to be at the center or the cause of a toxic situation.

While I'd like to say that I feel that I accomplished some sort of moral high ground in leaving, in retrospect, all I really accomplished by doing what I did was not benefit from no longer helping him. There's some solace and vindication in knowing that person was fired six months later. That I had played no part in his downfall aside from walking away and no longer covering up that incompetence made me feel a little better... but it had come at a high price.

Because when you leave a position like that, you don't just leave a job—you leave a culture and a network of people. Everyone you thought were your friends gradually just disappear when they realize you are no longer of any use to them professionally. It saddened me to realize that my friends no longer had time for lunch or drinks to the point I just stopped trying to book time with them. I might have somehow been able to get my foot back in at another studio eventually, but as those relationships rapidly dried up, so did my urge to try and get back into it.

The dream of being a Hollywood writer was now dead and gone. I walked away from it. Thus, as I pursued a non-Hollywood career, I returned to pursuing more intentionally my original dream. I was adrift in my career so I really needed to find my Prince Charming.

Shortly before leaving Disney, I had begun experimenting with the world of online dating. It's not like my profession the past several years had offered me the opportunity to meet many straight, single men.

Back then, most of the men you met on those sites were techies, IT guys who spent their lives on computers. The first guy I met in-person seemed like an internet dating success! He wooed me and at first made me feel good about myself. Tall, good looking—and controlling. Soon it was the little things: the car I drove wasn't cool enough. Over dinner one night he informed me that he could see where one day I'd need plastic surgery on my eyelids because he could tell where they were going to droop. He told me how to organize my apartment. Better yet, got me to move into a different apartment that was newer and more expensive when I got a new job as a writer and designer for a real estate marketing firm. Over New Year's, the millennium to be exact, he came with me to visit my parents in Nebraska.

I was shocked, honestly, that he wanted to come home with me over the holidays. I didn't realize we were quite that serious.

Turns out, we weren't. We got back and a few days later he called to inform me he was on his way to Palm Springs to spend the weekend with a girl he'd met that he had so much in common with. She drove a red Mustang convertible, like he did.

He was dumping me for a girl with the right car.

Truth be told, I had never been sure what he'd seen in me to begin with. I think ultimately he enjoyed that I took him to San Francisco with me to attend the *Toy Story 2* premiere. Once I left Disney, however, I apparently lost my usefulness. Like I had become to so many of my industry friends, I was no longer of any use. I was still in the middle of switching jobs and had not yet moved into the new apartment that he'd convinced me to get when he dumped me for Mustang girl.

Shortly after that was another IT guy. Another online find. Said all the right things. I was amazing. I was everything he'd dreamt of. Our first date went so well, talking until all hours of the night about our common interests. I was still, at my core, a science fiction and fantasy geek. So was he. Not to mention he reminded me of a blonder and better-looking version of Nicholas Cage.

Then, oops, several weeks in it turns out he was still living with his former girlfriend.

I drew the line and refused to date someone who was still living with his so-called "ex" girlfriend.

So, there was that. I did, sort of, have standards.

Eventually, he kicked her out and we resumed our relationship. I still was convinced this was the man I was going to marry, that we were destined to be together.

That's when the little things started. It was my fault that he no longer got to see the ex-girlfriend's daughter who had become like his daughter since he'd raised her for seven years. I was the cause of that resentment, naturally.

Then came the confession that he'd lied about having a college degree. He still made a good living in IT, but he thought I wouldn't date him if I knew he'd never finished college. And wouldn't I be just the total elitist bitch if I let that get in the way?

So I let it go.

Then he told me about the week he'd spent in jail for assault, years before we met, of course.

I told myself, this wasn't the first guy I'd dated that had spent time in jail. That first boyfriend in college: shoplifting. The Iranian guy I'd dated for a time while working at Disney Interactive had also spent a week in jail for shoplifting.

It was becoming a norm. People made mistakes. You couldn't hold that against them forever. It was in the past. I suppose I should have maybe seen all that as a red flag—none of those guys turned out to be gems and maybe instead of just normalizing it, I should have realized the common denominator. Instead, I normalized it and decided it was no big deal.

Little lies. Big lies. That all kept trickling out and I, being compassionate and in love, forgave. Forgave and forgave and forgave.

At least he wasn't cheating on me.

Instead, he was simply manipulating me. Things were always twisted around so that if I broke it off, I was the crappy person for not understanding "why" he'd lied. For not being forgiving. For not understanding. After all, look at everything he'd given up to be with me! He'd lost the girl he thought of as his daughter just to be with me. That's how much he loved me.

Six months later, the temper emerged. That getting arrested for assault thing maybe had some merit.

I found myself terrified by the bouts of anger that would burst forth. Threats to get out of the car and smash in someone's windshield when they cut him off in traffic; gunning it through the Wendy's drive-thru when the "stupid" minimum wage worker taking his order pissed him off. Throwing me up against a wall.

When I got scared enough, I would tell him to leave. Then he'd apologize. I stayed with him because he still told me all the things I wanted to hear. That I was worth any sacrifices he had to make.

I was so beautiful and intelligent—and he loved me.

Then came my twenty-eighth birthday.

I had just walked into my apartment after work excited about packing for our trip that we were taking to Santa Barbara that weekend, and then stopped dead in my tracks.

Something smelled bad.

The whiff of what could only have been the distinctive smell of cat shit hit my nostrils. I wrinkled my nose and went in search of the culprit. I was checking the litter box, corners, rooms, trying to figure out where she'd made her mess before I picked her up and realized the toxic goo was emanating from the cat herself, smeared and matted into the fur around her derriere.

Grabbing some paper towels, I attempted to clean the cat shit up. This was what I was doing when he walked into my apartment as I was standing there, holding the cat, when he decided right then was the appropriate time to drop his bombshell.

"I'm breaking up with you. Don't call me, I won't call you. You just aren't as smart as I thought you were." With that, he walked out the door and out of my life.

It was simply...over.

And there I stood, holding the white, furry cat with shit smeared all over her ass in one hand with the feces-covered paper towel I had been trying to clean it up with in the other, trying hard to ignore both the stench of the cat shit as well as the stench of being told that your boyfriend had decided you just "weren't as smart as I thought you were," and with that bids you adieu.

This is how a girl always wants to be remembered by the man who walks out her door for the last time. Holding a shit-covered cat with a shocked expression on her face.

Happy fucking birthday to me.

Sad part was, at some level I felt he was right. I had always warned him not to put me up on a pedestal. I was bound to fall off. I suffered from imposter syndrome and as intelligent as others seemed to think I was, I knew better. Plus, how did a smart person not break up with his ass months ago? That alone was a testament to my stupidity in my view.

It didn't matter that on one level I knew he had never been good for me. That didn't help the pain of the reality that I still loved him despite that. I was a wreck for some time after this, and I fell into a deep depression.

Yes, I was even to the point of being suicidal. I just wanted the pain and hurt of my broken heart to stop.

By this time, I had started working for an online mortgage company as their marketing director. The money wasn't bad, but it was hardly rewarding work. So not only had I lost the man I really thought I was going to one day marry, but I also no longer had the career I'd moved to California for in the first place. Both dreams lay in shambles.

What was the point in living when you see no future for yourself?

Eventually, one day, I fell on my knees in the kitchen and began considering all the different ways I could off myself. Slitting my wrists: too painful and bloody. Hanging? Nothing strong enough to hold me. The light fixtures would probably pull out of the ceiling and then I'd have to pay to replace them and repair the ceiling. Overdose? What if I wound up a vegetable?

Getting drunk in the car and letting the carbon monoxide put me to sleep so I'd never wake up? No garage.

It was probably a really good thing I didn't own a gun.

Instead, I fell on the kitchen floor, curled up into a little ball and begged God to either take the pain away or just to let me die, since I clearly didn't have the nerve to take my own life.

Now, as noted earlier, I was not overly religious at this juncture in my life. I didn't attend church, but I did read the Bible and had a fascination with religion and ancient cultures. Still, praying to God on the regular wasn't exactly my jam. God seemed to not have a lot of use for me, nor did I really for him. I'd only attended church as a teenager because my mother went, and I felt sorry that she had to attend alone as my dad had stopped going after we left the small rural church when I was about ten. Still, I had always found Biblical Studies fascinating. That had actually been evident even during my Disney days. One of my friends who worked up in the Pixar studios sent me scripts like *Dogma* to read before they were released just because she knew I had an interest in spiritual things. So while I had faith, it was not always as orthodox as many would like. I messed around with Tarot cards, experimented with more New Age-type religious beliefs, but nothing quite seemed to fit.

Yet, here I was curled up on the floor, begging for this God that I thought maybe existed to help me, because I saw nothing worth living for in my life.

That's when it happened. There was a "voice"—no, not like a booming from the burning bush type of voice out of a Charlton Heston movie—but that "still small voice" kind of thing that simply said, "Don't worry. I have other plans for you. But you need to move out of L.A." Then it felt like a warm blanket had been wrapped around me.

I immediately stopped crying, called my parents, and to their joy and elation, I told them I was moving back to Nebraska. Mom offered to come out and help me pack.

Just like that.

I know it sounds crazy, but I knew beyond a shadow of a doubt this was what I needed to be doing, and that it was the right thing to do. Somehow, things would work out. No clue how, but I just knew I needed to leave.

The next day I walked into the president of my division's office and told him I quit, I was moving back to Nebraska.

He leaned back in his chair and regarded me thoughtfully as I shifted uncomfortably in my seat. I liked my boss. He was a pretty nice guy overall.

Finally, he spoke: "Do you have another job?"

I shook my head. "No."

"So you're not moving back for a better job then?"

I shook my head again and repeated, "No. I'm moving back for personal reasons. I just feel I need to move home and be closer to family."

He considered this for a moment, then leaned forward, peering at me over his steepled fingers that were pressed against his lips.

"Then why are you quitting?"

I looked at him, confused. Had he not heard me?

"I mean, it's not like you don't email me everything you do anyway, and you only sit ten feet outside my office," he continued. "I see no reason why you can't just email me your work from Nebraska instead of here."

So he sent me to Nebraska with a computer and a California salary with Nebraska's cost of living. I bought a home in Lincoln, and for the next three years, I would telecommute to Pasadena from Lincoln in my role as a marketing director for a mortgage company.

During this time those "other plans" that voice warned me about began to take shape.

September 11th happened a few months after I returned to Nebraska. So many lives changed that day, including mine. While we lost a family friend that day, something deeper within me altered. I began seriously re-evaluating my own life and choices. We lived in a dangerous world and the reality of my own mortality loomed large.

I began reassessing my life and looking back over all the things I was doing. Sure, I now was fairly well-established in my job and career as a graphic designer and marketing director. My next step would have been to move on to vice president, which came with more money and more headaches and stress.

I began asking if that's what I really wanted in life? What was after vice president? I would never be president of the division because I had zero clue about mortgages aside from how to market them, and it wasn't exactly something I cared to know more about.

As I approached thirty years old, I still had zero real prospects for fulfilling my childhood dream of a husband and children. I had my career, and that was it. A career that required I get up each morning and walk from my bedroom to my other bedroom that served as my office.

That was it. That was my life. I got up each day and made fliers to sell mortgage products so I could make an already too-rich CEO richer. Mortgage products that seemed...off. I began asking questions like why were we offering no-documentation, no down payment loans to people alongside Adjustable Rate Mortgages? All of those things seemed like really bad ideas.

I was told no; this just made it much easier for people who were self-employed to get mortgages. It was a good thing. I just didn't understand how the industry really worked.

In other words, I got told to stay in my lane.

I don't know that I need say much further when I say that the already too-rich CEO I was working for happened to be the CEO of Countrywide lending—one of the top culprits of the 2008 financial crash. He never spent a day in jail, and I recently read he passed away this past year. He was responsible for destroying millions of lives and aside from a sixty million dollar fine he easily paid and being barred from ever serving on the board of any publicly traded company ever again; that was the extent of punishment he endured.

Call it an early penance, but years before the financial crash, I found myself being drawn to the church my mother worked at as the Chief Financial Officer. I guess deep down I just knew what I was doing and who I was working for was no good.

Again, I had never been an overly religious person, and still really wasn't. Oh sure, I'd picked up my life and moved halfway across the country because

I was pretty sure a voice from God had told me to, but other than that, things had been pretty quiet on that front.

But in this quest for trying to figure out my life, becoming more aware of my own mortality, I began asking questions like, "If I died today, what would I have to show for my life? If I have to stand before God and give an accounting for my life, what would I tell him? I made rich people richer?"

Somehow, that didn't sound like the kind of life that would be considered "worthy" by anyone's definitions. Especially not some all-powerful deity who got to judge my life.

I had started leading Bible studies, forming some young adult groups, and eventually the pastor began talking to me about going to seminary.

The notion was both ridiculous—and intriguing. I did love to study theology and religion.

But a pastor? That part seemed rather laughable. I'd worked in Hollywood, after all. I was not exactly a paragon of virtue, nor did I have any moral standing to try and tell others how to live their lives.

Apparently, that would make a very effective pastor, or so I was told.

I began rattling off all the excuses I could think of.

I had no desire to move that far away from my family ever again.

Oh, but didn't my brother live in the Twin Cities? There just happened to be a seminary in St. Paul.

Well, I couldn't really afford to go in that kind of debt at this point in my life. I was, after all, in my thirties now.

Oh, hey, the church has a scholarship fund and will take care of my tuition for me.

I loved my house. I wasn't ready to just up and leave my house.

Over the next two weeks, my sprinkler system sprang a leak and flooded my basement, along with a series of other events that made me begin to question my decision to be a homeowner.

Suffice it to say, I eventually was convinced to go visit the seminary, and as I sat in the middle of one of the classes there was once again this "voice" that told me I was where I belonged. So, I sold my house and moved to St. Paul, Minnesota to attend seminary.

My search for Prince Charming was indefinitely put on hold. I thought dating before was rough? Try being a female pastor.

Three
In God's Hands

> *"It is in those times of hopeless chaos when the sovereign hand of God is most likely to be seen."*
>
> — Thomas Chalmers

GOING TO SEMINARY WASN'T me giving up on my dream of Prince Charming. Honestly, I thought maybe this was the direction God was leading me to find him. I still could not fathom that this God who told Adam, "it is not good to be alone" would leave me to be alone forever. I knew there would be new challenges with this new vocation, but maybe this was just honing me in on who I was supposed to be with.

Giving up on yet another career path to go back to school, move several hundred miles away again, and just place yourself in the hands of a God who seemed to be beckoning and calling you into this strange world of ministry is probably one of the greatest acts of faith I've ever taken. Well, I guess that and just up and moving to Los Angeles with no job lined up. Or, you know, that whole just leaving California because you think God told you to thing. At least here there was an educational structure and endgame to my studies. However, to this day, I laugh at the people who tell me how I'm "usurping God's will" by becoming a pastor and just following my "itching ears," as though this was a decision I made completely on my own because I just suddenly decided I needed to be a pastor.

Not only did I resist such a call, but even as I answered it, I still was not entirely sure this was what I was really supposed to be doing. Staying in parish ministry just didn't "fit" who I was very well. At least in my own view.

Fifteen years later, I still am not sure how I continued in the parish.

So I laugh at these people who think this is a life we choose for ourselves out of all the other things we could possibly be doing with our lives. Like, you know, making movies in Hollywood or something.

It's an utter act of faith where we lay ourselves bare before this deity who has set us on this journey.

We place ourselves "In God's Hands" because there is nothing else for us to do. We come before God stripped bare of everything. Everything is revealed. Our hurts, our pain, sorrow, and even our very future is put in his hands, as we are molded and shaped. We are but a mere part of the vast expanse of the cosmos, and yet, still molded and shaped by our Creator to be the specific people we are.

In order to become new creations through Jesus Christ, we are placed in the hands of God to be made new each and every day.

As it turns out, seminary was where I finally met "my people." I've always been something of a loner. I never made any real connections in California aside from the boyfriend who dumped me while I held my shit-covered cat. While social media has reconnected me with some of them years later, only one of them walked through some of my more recent struggles with me. I made lifelong friends in seminary, most of whom I still keep in some sort of contact with, again thanks to social media.

Still, the thought of being a pastor was not really at the forefront of my thoughts. Yes, I was going through ordination, but I really thought I'd maybe wind up going on at some point for my Ph.D., and parish ministry would become merely a steppingstone in that endeavor. Despite what my own pastor had said, I did not see myself as being particularly gifted in offering people care and support. The scholastic side of it, on the other hand, I absolutely loved.

Delving deep into people's problems? I wasn't sure I was cut out for that.

At the same time, my parents had always accused me of "taking in the strays" in terms of people. It's how they wound up taking in a foreign exchange student from Australia when I was in high school, because I felt sorry for and wanted to help her when things didn't work out with her host family. It's how they wound up providing shelter for a friend of mine who had called me up when I was in college saying her father was beating her. I drove out, picked her up, and because I lived in the dorms and couldn't take her back with me, took her to my parent's place.

My "toxic trait" is I want to help everyone who comes across my path that's in need. The frustrating part of being a pastor is that these people come to you expecting you can and will help them, and the resources are rarely there to do that. So people like me go into it with a desire to help, then get burned out and despondent when we realize we aren't able to meet the mounting needs that wind up on our doorstep each day. Which then makes them angry because we're the church; we're supposed to help. If you ever wonder why pastors leave the ministry, that's part of the problem. I mean, there's also the reality of dealing with toxic parishioners and abusive systems, but pastoral burnout is multi-faceted.

I also tended to be the person all of my friends came to with their problems. I didn't believe I was particularly adept at giving advice—my own life was not exactly full of the best choices. A string of terrible taste in men, and here I was on my third career at the tender age of thirty-one. But I did listen a lot and was able to express a certain amount of solidarity with whatever issue they were having.

That empathy is, I suppose, both what winds up making a decent pastor, and also what can so easily be manipulated by others.

I tend to also get burned by this when people come to me in need. I open up my compassion, give the benefit of the doubt, sometimes even bring people into my home. And at every turn, I will usually get burned for it somehow. Probably one of the most memorable situations was when I was on internship, a woman broke into my apartment while she was having a psychotic break and started knocking on my bathroom door while I was in the bathtub.

There is nothing more terrifying than standing naked in your shower and having someone knocking on your bathroom door when you live alone. Still, rather than call the police on her, I got dressed, listened to her problems, and then took her to the hospital and got her checked into the mental health unit.

Seminary itself, though, was both one of the best experiences of my life, and one of the most challenging. Academically I had no issues. I quickly rose to the top of my class grade-wise and gained a particular reputation as one of the "smart" students. However, it started out a bit on the rocky side.

When I first arrived, I, of course, knew no one. We had a week of orientation where we got to know some of our fellow students. I was grouped for a day of service with another woman about seven years or so younger than I was. We both kept giving each other strange looks, and then we both finally admitted that we thought we had met before. The closest we could come to figuring out where we might have known each other from was she had attended school at Midland College in Fremont, Nebraska—but I was living in California during her college years so that didn't jive, and she wasn't from Nebraska; she was from East Grand Forks, Minnesota on the North Dakota border. Eighteen years later, we've still never figured it out. Just one of those people we knew from "somewhere," and were perhaps simply destined to be in each other's lives.

Being the introvert that I was, I pretty much believed I was going to just go to class, come back to my little apartment and study constantly. And, for about the first week, that's pretty much what life was like.

My first day of classes, I immediately wondered if I hadn't made a terrible mistake selling my home, moving into this little one bedroom, nearly ghetto apartment. (The apartments had water marks on the walls from where they'd flooded in the past and were full of mold. Other students complained of rats and cockroaches, but luckily, I seemed to not have that problem.)

My very first class was called "Pentateuch." It was a class on the first five books of the Hebrew Bible. I was excited. Finally, some formal education on Biblical Studies. I was ready and eager to learn.

The white-haired professor came striding into the room, closed the door behind him and immediately announced:

"Don't ever go looking for Noah's Ark. It never happened."

I blinked rapidly.

I'm sorry, *what?*

He proceeded to tell us how the first eleven chapters of Genesis were "pre-history" and mythological in nature.

I blinked some more. Again, *what?*

Adam and Eve weren't real, just metaphors?

Noah's Ark never happened.

Tower of Babel was just metaphor and a play on words in the original Hebrew as well.

By the end of the class, I'd placed my head on my desk and wondered what on earth I'd done.

Upon returning to my apartment, I began to cry and throw things. This was seriously what I was going to be taught? I'd sold my house, moved into this moldy, cockroach-infested hell-hole for *this?*

There's a saying the professors use when you enter seminary: "We tear your faith down so we can build it back up."

Well, they were doing a bang-up job with that whole tearing down thing. Now it's not that I took everything in the narratives of Genesis literally to begin with. I had my own ideas regarding how evolution worked in the midst of the creation narrative, and while I doubted the story of Noah was recorded exactly the way it happened, I figured it was rooted in some sort of historical event. After all, every culture in the world had a flood story. Every religion had their own version.

So it seemed highly irresponsible if not downright arrogant to claim it never happened. After all, how could hundreds of different flood stories not be rooted in some sort of historical reality?

I seriously dreaded going to class again.

It would strangely be my Greek class where I would ultimately meet my small group of friends that I'd wind up spending most of my time in seminary with.

It started with a take-home exam where we were told to work on the test by ourselves. Okay, no problem. Languages came easily to me, and Greek was no different. I sat down and had the test done within an hour or so.

Later that evening, my phone rang. It was the girl from orientation who had gone to Midland and sat in front of me in our Greek class.

"Hey. So, I thought you might have the same kind of ethics I do about this take home test thing," she started off. I raised a curious eyebrow. Oh? She thought she knew my ethics, did she?

"Oh? And what ethics are those?" I responded.

"Yeah, so, I need help. Would you be willing to work on this together?"

I glanced over at my already finished exam and let out a sigh. "Yeah, sure," I said after a minute. "Come on over." She was right. It was in my nature to just help someone in need. It wasn't like I was going to just give her the answers. I was going to help her understand what she was doing.

So, she came over, I helped make things like the aorist tense make more sense to her, and when she left, she asked if I could help tutor her in Greek class. Again, I said sure; I'd meet her at the cafeteria the next morning.

So we met, and I bought her some hot chocolate. Now, primarily the reason I did that was I still was working my marketing job out in California part time, and I realized I probably had more money than many of my classmates. Buying someone's hot chocolate seemed like a nice gesture.

She started laughing at me and went, "Wait...so, you're helping me *and* you're buying my hot chocolate? Are you *that* desperate for friends?"

I let out a laugh, as I realized...yeah, actually, I was. I'd left Hollywood friendless, and working from home in Lincoln for the past three years for a company located in Pasadena had not exactly produced a lot of friendships back in Nebraska, either. I realized: I was lonely. I was thirty-one, single, and utterly alone.

I was starved for friendship, and I guess at some level I actually was trying to buy myself a friend.

So, I shrugged, handed her the hot cocoa and said, "Yup."

She stared at the cup of cocoa for a moment, then looked at me, also shrugged, and went, "Okay, cool. I can be bought for some hot chocolate."

We became fast friends after that. For the price of a cup of hot chocolate. Our little study sessions in the cafeteria after Greek class eventually began to grow as other classmates began to join us, and we soon became known as the "Greek Geeks" who sat around one of the cafeteria tables every day after class talking about, you guessed it, Greek.

I'd inadvertently found my people. We frequently discussed this whole "tearing our faith down," thing that the professors were dedicated to doing. The building it back up part? That's the element that seemed to be missing.

I realize now it's what many would refer to as "deconstructing" your faith. We lamented how often we seemed to get told nothing we once thought actually happened in the Bible really probably happened.

It took time to realize the difference between truth versus historical fact, and that scripture was interested in spiritual truths—not necessarily historical realities. That metaphors could carry an even deeper understanding of God and our world than most literal events ever could.

Still, it was not easy, and it created some seismic shifts in not just my faith, but my entire worldview. The repercussions of that over a decade later are still getting played out in my life. It's made me look at people of other faiths differently. It's made me look at a whole slew of social issues differently. I came out of seminary a very different person.

Now don't get me wrong, this created a much deeper, more nuanced, and beautiful faith than I had possessed before. It just would take being in my ministry setting for me to begin to recognize that. So I wouldn't say seminary rebuilt my torn down understandings, but having to use what I learned in the "real world" definitely did.

Seminary taught me a lot of things beyond just Biblical scholarship. It taught me how systems protect themselves. It taught me even in church there were a lot of agendas at play. It showed me many of the darker elements of organized religion.

It also taught me a lot about what an authentic, caring, Christian community *could* look like.

In March of 2006, I received a phone call from my father that started off with, "We're okay, but we crashed the plane." Apparently, they had been on their way to California and stopped for fuel in Winslow, Arizona. The engine died on take-off when they were only about two hundred feet in the air. Somehow, my father managed to steer the plane out over the desert, and they crash-landed away from a populated area. Not only did they manage to walk away from it virtually unharmed, with the exception of some scrapes and cuts from the barbed-wire fence they became tangled in trying to get out of the plane, but not a single bottle of my father's homebrew beer he was taking to their Palm Springs home had broken. Which then resulted in a very drunken phone call around midnight when they got out of the hospital and to their hotel because the only thing they'd gotten to eat that day following the crash was some cheese in their cooler and the beer.

I found myself going through what I could only refer to as "reverse shock." I knew they were alive, and they were fine, but still, the reality of what they had just escaped hit me like a ton of bricks as I knew how close I had come to losing them that day.

I was supposed to take a worship terms exam in class the next day. For the first time in my seminary career, I flunked a test. My brain simply had not recovered from the shock of the previous day. Fortunately, when I spoke to the instructor, they said my grades were good enough and there was no need to retake the test. Unfortunately, to this day if you ask me what the proper names are for all the items we use in worship, I'll likely still call it "that square cardboard thingy." (Luckily, I don't think God cares that I don't know the name of that square cardboard thingy.)

Then my best friend (the one who I bought for the price of a hot chocolate) and I were in a car accident that following June. We were T-boned at an intersection by a car running a red light and smashing into the passenger side where I was sitting. It would take me months to walk normally again, and I still believe that accident contributed to my cervical spine and disc issues I would start having a few years later. (That, and roller coasters.)

For the first time in my adult life, however, I did not go through these things alone. I had my other seminary classmates and friends who were there to help care for me and support me. I learned that this was what Christian community was *supposed* to be like. This was what caring about each other and loving your neighbor *could* mean.

I would find out in that "real world" of ministry that there are indeed pockets of authentic Christian community that will sustain you, and systems within those same communities that might nearly destroy you. Yet, in this moment and time, they were what I needed.

After four years of seminary, I graduated and was assigned back to the Nebraska Synod. The call process would take another several months. During that time period, I moved back in with my parents as signing a lease for an apartment didn't seem wise when I had no idea how long or short the process was going to be. Eight months after I was assigned to Nebraska, I was finally ordained, and nine months after that I finally was able to start my new call and move out of my parent's place.

Word to the wise: I do not recommend moving back in with your parents while in your mid-thirties.

Still, this was not the fairy tale I had envisioned for my life. Thirty-six years old and I was moving to a town of thirty-thousand people—as a pastor of all things. After Los Angeles, Minneapolis, and even Lincoln which at least had a quarter of a million people, a town of thirty thousand seemed to be a death sentence on the notion that I would ever find my Prince Charming. Time was rapidly running out, as my gynecologist put it, if I had any hope of still having that family I so desperately desired.

Where on earth was my Prince Charming? I somehow doubted he was wandering the streets of Kearney, Nebraska.

Four
The Compromise

"Compromise is but the sacrifice of one right or good in the hope of retaining another—too often ending in the loss of both."

— Tryon Edwards

RARELY DO FAIRY TALES focus on what happens when the Princess marries the wrong Prince Charming. Oh, sure, *Beauty and the Beast* had Gaston as a buffoon of a suitor, and the Beast seemed like a self-centered narcissist, though through the course of the story he transforms—physically and emotionally—into a different person. The prince in the original *Little Mermaid* falls for and marries the wrong woman, though we don't really ever get the sense that the wrong woman was an abusive, narcissistic demon. Probably the closest I've found to this was in Disney's *Frozen* which had the evil narcissistic prince who tried to woo Anna into marrying him only hours after meeting him. Having lived such an isolated life, she immediately fell for him, and it almost destroyed her. *Frozen* aside, few fairy tales explore what happens when you fall in love with the wrong prince. They rarely go down the road of "Princess so desperate to get married to Prince Charming, she falls in love with Prince Not-So-Charming."

Yet this type of fairy tale was my reality.

It was a warm June summer evening as I slid onto the stool of the Old Chicago located on Second Avenue in the bustling metropolis of Kearney, Nebraska. I ordered a glass of red wine, and, in what I know screamed "irresistible woman sitting at the bar," I pulled out a book I'd been reading as part of my sermon prep. I sat there and sipped my wine, glancing occasionally up from the book to the television that hung on the wall above the shelves of liquor. Poker was on.

June: the doldrums of sporting seasons.

There was a rather loud, flannel-clad truck driver-type sitting at the other end flirting with the female bartender. He was younger and thinner than most drivers I came across, a nondescript worn yellowish baseball cap covered a protrusion of greasy-blond hair that curled up under the edges. I was busy ignoring their conversation as I delved back into my book on stewardship.

Yawn.

It didn't take long for me to think Texas Hold'em poker on ESPN was more interesting.

I sighed.

Was this going to be the rest of my life? Sitting at the local pub watching poker with the bartender and the clearly drunk flannel-clad truck driver? Either that or sitting at home with my cat while drinking wine, reading a book, and watching some equally brain-deadening reality show on television? Okay, I hate reality TV, but that's all that was on before the streaming option for Netflix came along.

The only reason I was sitting alone in a bar reading a book while drinking wine was because even for an introvert like myself, I knew engaging occasionally in some form of normal-ish human interaction was helpful.

It wasn't like I didn't know this was the path I was on, that I hadn't gone in with both eyes wide open knowing that my social life, such that it had been, was going to take a full-on header into the toilet when I determined I was supposed to go to seminary. We make choices in life. This was one—I knew the consequences.

I thought I was okay with the consequences. I thought ministry would be an all-consuming, completely fulfilling path that would make my singleness somehow seem less lonely.

Quite the opposite occurred. Pastors are, by nature, isolated. We can't develop close friendships with our parishioners due to keeping appropriate boundaries so as not to abuse our positions of perceived power. Our lives become fishbowls, and every move we make is the topic of congregational gossip.

Knowing it and experiencing the reality are sometimes two different things. There was some part of me that I think thought: *well, maybe I'll meet someone in seminary.* Clergy couples were a thing. Or so I'd heard. Alas, I managed four years and only resulted in twice being sexually harassed by classmates that resulted in other people making reports on my behalf after witnessing their creepy behavior toward me.

Reality was, I didn't even realize I'd been sexually harassed. I had become so accustomed to just being treated like garbage by men, it didn't register as anything out of the ordinary.

I'd been asked by the dean of students if I wanted to pursue discipline in each case. Each time I declined. It didn't seem worth it.

In retrospect, I regret that decision. I should have pursued it as those men are now serving in congregations where they are likely behaving just as badly.

As poker droned on above me, I drained the fermented grape juice and lifted the empty glass up, indicating to the bartender that I'd have a refill. She popped the cork off the house wine and topped me off.

"I'll get that one," said Flannel-boy at the end of the bar.

Perfect. Now I'm going to get hit on by the drunk driver. I smiled appreciatively anyway, because that's what you do. You smile and say thank you when someone does something nice. Even when you know what the result of your perfunctory gratitude will be.

Yup. Sure enough, he moseyed over to the stool next to me and gave me a tobacco-stained grin. His left incisor was missing, and he smelled like whiskey and cigarettes.

I hated whiskey. Ever since I was twelve and my dad gave me a shot of Jack Daniels one afternoon because I was curious about what he and my mom were drinking every night, I now associated the foul stuff with a burning throat and fits of coughing. Guess that whole philosophy of give a kid a pack of cigarettes and making them smoke it in one sitting worked with certain forms of alcohol, too. Although, sneaking a few glasses of mimosas one Christmas and getting unwittingly trashed at the same age didn't deter me from drinking champagne and orange juice going forward. Heck, I wasn't even deterred after twelve glasses of champagne in fifteen minutes on New Year's Eve when I was twenty-two that resulted in not only my hair swirling in the toilet of the bathroom at the bar I worked at, but the next morning my continuing to puke in the snow in the parking lot as my mom quietly brushed the piles of white flakes off my car to cover the brown vomit.

So much for that theory.

Hated cigarettes, too. Too many nights I went to bed smelling like an ashtray from the aforementioned bar I worked at during college. Exhausting evenings of swishing my hips and stuffing socks in my bra to make my breasts look bigger than they were to get those couple of extra bucks in tips. I still remember one of my co-workers laughing hysterically when after work one night we were sitting in my apartment and I pulled the rolled-up socks out, tossing them across the room.

They also smelled like an ashtray.

Then my pillow and sheets would smell, and oh yeah, there was the time I had a nicotine-fit after taking three days off from work. Secondhand smoke was awesome. Especially when mingled with whiskey.

Flannel-boy started chatting, the stink of the cigarettes and whiskey expelling with every word he spoke. I laughed, smiled, added to whatever the conversation was that I don't even remember at this point and fought every instinct to cough and wave rudely to try and dispel the whiskey-tobacco breath. He complimented me on my long red hair and blue eyes. I gave a cursory thank you. Eventually he talked about how he was from Denver and drove a truck for a living and had just stopped for the night.

Didn't see *that* coming. (Eyeroll dripping with sarcasm.)

"So what do you do?" he asked, that brown-laced grin widening.

My smile broadened. *Oh, now for the* real *fun.*

Without missing a beat, I responded, "Oh, I'm a pastor."

On cue: grin faded, replaced by shocked expression.

"Holy shit! What the fuck? Really? No. You're shitting me, right?"

The bartender's eyes widened. "Dude," she said in exasperation, "she just told you she's a pastor and your reaction is to *swear* at her?"

I successfully fought the giggle, but my smile remained plastered on my face.

"Oh, fuck, shit...like, I'm sorry," he stammered.

I bit back a guffaw as the bartender rolled her eyes and shook her head. The flush in his face deepened as he stumbled through a few more profanity-laced attempts at an apology before he eventually found an excuse to disentangle himself from the conversation and headed to the bathroom. When he returned, it was to resume his seat at the other end of the bar.

Well, I figured that was enough entertainment for one night. I closed my book and paid my bill, walking out into the warm early summer evening. I breathed in deeply, the pungent excrement-laden odor of the feedlot that we sat downwind from filling my nostrils.

Oh, the symbolism.

Arriving home, I tossed my keys on the table that sat against the wall just inside my front door. Tiki, my part Tabby, part Siamese cat jumped on the back of the recliner to greet me. I reached out and scratched behind her ears as she nuzzled her soft nose against my hand. Then suddenly, she nipped at me and jumped off the chair to go running full-speed into the kitchen.

I rolled my eyes.

Freaking psycho cat.

Yup, that's me. Pathetic, pastor, psycho-cat lady.

I flopped into the burgundy recliner and flipped on the television, then flipped it back off a few minutes later. Apparently poker really was the best thing on TV that night.

I pulled out my laptop and stared at the blinking cursor in Microsoft Word for several moments. That's as far as I'd gotten on my sermon for the weekend. Maybe Facebook had something more interesting to tell me.

Oh look, mom was online. Maybe she wanted to chat.

I love my mom, and as the vomit-covering-with-snow incident alluded to, she's pretty awesome and amazing. So don't take this the wrong way, but: I burst into tears.

It wasn't that I cared all that much about the encounter with the truck driver at the bar. He wasn't remotely my type, so there was nothing I was missing out on there. In fact, I really had found the entire encounter rather amusing.

However, it was as though his response summed up in the perfect caricature every reaction I received when I told people I was a pastor. His was just more honest and blatant.

Thank you Jim Beam.

I mean, it wasn't as though I hadn't had a hard enough time in the dating world prior to becoming a pastor; I thought I'd just throw that extra little bit of challenge in there for kicks and giggles.

Blowing my nose and wiping my tears, determined not to make the evening a pity party about how depressing my life was—and was seemingly destined to remain—I logged into my email account. I had new responses to my online dating profile. You'd think I'd have learned my lesson with the kind of men I wound up dating due to the online dating medium, but no. It still seemed the only avenue for me to meet single men.

Oh, this should be fun, I thought with that mingled sense of both hope and dread. Most inquiries to my profile were either guys I had zero interest in or were ones that as soon as they found out what I did for a living would run the other direction. Either the whole concept of dating someone "of the cloth" freaked them out because they just "weren't that religious," or they were super-religious to the point that they thought that as a woman I really shouldn't be a pastor.

Thank you, sexism.

In fact, there was a reply from a nice, so-called "faith-filled" guy in my inbox this evening. I clicked open the response and read, not for the first time, all the reasons he couldn't deal with a woman who was "usurping the Word of God," "following her itching ears," because "the man should be the spiritual leader of the household," and didn't I know that a "woman was not permitted to teach a man?"

Delete.

Years later, my therapist would tell me that I had a "false narrative" in my head about how men just didn't want to date a woman pastor.

She clearly never read those emails.

False narrative or not, it was the narrative I had. The pattern of men I had dated in my life all had some pretty common denominators. Controlling. Cheating. Anger management issues.

One day, I received an email back from an online dating prospect who, when he discovered I was a pastor, didn't tell me I was usurping God's Word by doing what I did. Nor did he balk at the notion in terms of being fearful that I was too "holier than thou." He seemed genuinely interested in what I did, and not in a weird fetishized "are you a naughty pastor?" "I'd like to see you in your collar and nothing else," kind of thing I sometimes ran into.

I realize that was a pretty low bar, but it's where I was at.

For the first time in a decade, I had a glimmer of hope. I clung to it. Did I dare think this could be someone who would accept me for who I was? Could I really have found someone who would truly love me?

A lot of thoughts for someone I'd never met.

We continued to chat for about two more months. It was a different time when you didn't just swipe left or right on someone's picture. You actually talked with each other and got to know the other person to some degree before you met them. He had a sixteen-year-old daughter and that made me a little nervous. I'd never dated anyone with kids before because kids were complicated. They always came as part of a messy situation, and trying to come in as an authority figure of some sort I just knew was not my forté. I always believed that if I had kids of my own—I would have been a good mother. But being a parent to someone else's child? Well...

But I was thirty-eight years old.

And, as the bar incident had proven, my profession did not make me a desirable catch in the eyes of most men—not even the greasy truck-driver types. He was a refreshing change. Someone who didn't seem scared of what I did for a living. Oh, he had questions. We had some disagreements and debates, but overall he seemed to accept me for who and what I was. More than that, he encouraged me. He supported what I was doing.

So, he had a sixteen-year-old daughter? So what? A few years left in the house and she'd be off to college or whatever, and no big deal, right?

Tick. Tick. Tick.

That was my biological clock kicking into high gear as I still remembered the words of that gynecologist I had seen a few years earlier: "If you are going to have kids, you really should get started."

Thanks for that newsflash.

The big 4-0 was looming ever closer. I was still spouseless and childless, and this was the first real prospect I'd gone out with in over ten years. I didn't have another ten years in me to wait around for the next possibility.

"No one's perfect," I kept telling myself. Everyone has baggage, everyone has flaws, and some of that baggage involves the teenage variety.

Tick. Tick. Tick.

The downside, he lived three hours away in Omaha, so it wasn't like we could just go grab a drink and meet. It required some coordination. Plus, we had started talking in the middle of the holidays, so it wasn't the easiest time in the world to try and make our schedules work.

Eventually, we would meet, however.

Two days after I turned thirty-eight, I found myself sitting anxiously at the bar at Misty's Steakhouse in the Havelock district of Lincoln.

I'd had a doctor's appointment to deal with my spine issues earlier in the day, had driven in from Kearney, and planned to spend the night at my parents' house. He was driving in from Omaha.

I'd ordered a rum and Diet Coke, as though that diet portion would somehow offset the calories in the rum. Oh yes, I still had weight issues.

He was shorter than I imagined. I'm not sure why I thought five-foot-nine would somehow be taller than it was. Then of course, no one ever looks exactly like you imagine they will, even when you've seen pictures.

Still, who was I to judge height, standing at just five-foot-three and three-quarters myself. (That three-quarters of an inch is important!) When people make short jokes, I typically understand all too well what they're talking about. He was still taller than me, so what did it matter? It didn't. It just wasn't completely what I was expecting for some reason.

He wore a long black trench coat and black leather gloves and looked quite dashing—is that a word that is still used to describe handsome men? Dashing?

He had dark hair with light wisps of gray caused by his sixteen-year-old daughter, he claimed.

"You drive a Buick?" he said with a certain amount of amusement in his voice as he approached me at the bar where I was sipping—oh, who am I kidding, I don't sip, I gulp—my rum and Diet Coke.

I cringed. Of course he figured out what car was mine. Nebraska had a unique system of using numbers on their license plates to identify what county you lived in. Amidst all the clearly Lincoln and Omaha plates, my nine-county had to have stuck out like a sore thumb.

As did my 1997 Buick LeSabre, which was a great car...for grandma. Clearly now would not be the time to confess that prior to that granny vehicle I'd been driving my mother's old car, a 1988 Chrysler New Yorker. That had been the car that I had owned when the controlling dude who told me I'd need surgery on my eyelids one day, dumped me for red Mustang girl. The old Chrysler just wasn't "cool" enough.

He had a point.

Droopy eyelid guy aside, my cars had always been paid for and faithfully transported me from point A to point B, and that was what mattered most. Still, I had flashbacks to that moment of being told I was being dumped over a car and felt a twinge of panic rising in my stomach.

"Don't judge the car," I said, trying to keep my cheeks from flushing. Ugh. I hated my red cheeks. Especially after I'd already had a drink. That darn Scottish and German ancestry always crept up on me. No matter how much make-up I applied, my face always managed to have the coloring of a drunk Irishman.

He gave me a strange smile that didn't quite reveal his teeth.

I fully admit, it was not what I would call love at first sight. There was something that seemed—off about him, though I was never able to fully put my finger on it. Still, nothing that was off-enough for me to end the date and never see him again.

We ordered wine with our prime rib dinner and the conversation flowed easily from topics of movies we liked to stories about his teenage daughter. I found it appalling he'd never seen any Monty Python movies, and as dinner came to a close, he suggested that rather than parting ways immediately, we go rent a copy of the *Holy Grail*, since he'd never seen it. Streaming had not quite hit the marketplace yet, so video stores were still a thriving business.

We made our way to the nearest Blockbuster and per his suggestion, rented *Monty Python's Quest for the Holy Grail* and went back to my parents' place to watch it.

It felt almost like I was in high school again, having a boy over to watch movies while the parents were gone. Only I never really did that in high school because, well, I never really dated in high school. Still, it had a certain feeling like I was doing something I shouldn't be. Something about that at thirty-eight years old kind of thrilled me for some reason.

When the movie was over, I saw him to my parents' door, where he gave me a quick kiss goodnight and said he'd call me to set up another date.

Sure enough, I awoke the next morning to a text message telling me he'd really enjoyed our date and he'd like to take me out again if I made it out this way or maybe he could come to Kearney.

I hesitated on the last suggestion. Remember, as a pastor, I lived in a fishbowl. People always up in my business. Omaha was safer. I'd just make the drive for the time being.

Our second date involved an evening at Dave and Buster's. It had been snowing heavily, and I didn't want to get on the roads and drive the three hours back to Kearney so I wound up staying the night in a spare room at his house. The next morning when I got up to leave, I turned my car on—and immediately heard the offending sound of *"It's a Small World After All"* blaring through my car speakers.

I immediately began to laugh.

His daughter loved Disney movies, and I had made a point to tell him how much I never, ever, wanted to hear *"It's a Small World After All"* again for as long as I lived. My years working for Disney had caused me to despise that song after hearing it as hold music constantly and of course at Disneyland, where I went too often because as employees, we were always given free tickets.

I suppose that's the moment where I began to really begin thinking this might turn into an actual, legitimate relationship. Between the fact that he had wanted to watch a movie I loved, and had paid enough attention to things I said I liked and disliked that he went to the trouble of burning a CD with that accursed song on it and slipping it into my car's CD player in the middle of the night, I began to realize that he was really paying attention to the things I told him about myself. Even if they were being used in a cute way to torture me. I mean, there were other songs on that CD.

He'd made me the millennial edition of a Gen X mixed tape.

What should have been my first red flag, however, was on about our third or fourth date. I was on my way to Omaha and was about thirty minutes away from the restaurant when he called and informed me that his sixteen-year-old daughter and his best friend were both going to be joining us for dinner.

I nearly turned around and drove the three hours back home right then and there. The thought of meeting his daughter already at this stage of the relationship seemed way too soon. We'd even discussed how I shouldn't meet her until we were a little more certain of where this relationship was headed.

I began to panic.

What if she didn't like me? What if I didn't like her?

My worst fears were realized as I walked into the restaurant and sat down. His daughter was a beautiful girl—who was also sullen, rude, self-absorbed, and clearly had no interest in me. There was absolutely nothing we had in common with the exception of her father. She wasn't your normal teenage moody, either. The level of rudeness and disrespect was like nothing I'd ever encountered.

Was I about to jump from the role of the Princess to the evil stepmother? Without ever getting to be the Princess first? That hardly seemed fair.

I'd never related well to children to begin with, certainly not moody teenagers. I used to joke that I never got along well with teenage girls, even when I was one. I found nothing they had to talk about of interest, typically. Clothing, music, boys—none of these were things I cared much about. I was the weird sci-fi/fantasy-reading geek turned pastor. Nothing cool about that.

Well, ok, maybe I had interest in boys. But I clearly had no frame of reference for dating at sixteen. That wasn't in my experience. I didn't have boys falling over themselves trying to date me.

I knew immediately I was going to be the most hated girlfriend her father had ever dated.

Still, I tried. I did what I could to feign interest in whatever she seemed to like at the moment, but kids can sense bullshit from a mile away, and I was certain I was exuding it by the truckload.

I was nearly in tears by the time I drove home later that evening. Not only did I feel blindsided by the impromptu meeting with his daughter, but I'd also had to meet his best friend of nine years.

That went a little better as he seemed to genuinely like and approve of me.

I was pretty well convinced at that point that no relationship with him could possibly work given the daughter came with the package. I didn't really see a way past that until she at least graduated from high school in another year.

Which meant a year of trying to navigate our way through a long-distance relationship.

I should have listened to that instinct as the daughter rapidly became a point of contention in our relationship, because I simply wasn't equipped to deal with the drama she created.

Still, he began wanting to talk to me about his struggles with her, and even confided that he thought she might have some kind dissociative disorder. Her mother was bi-polar and a drug addict that was constantly in and out of rehab. I chalked a huge part of her behavioral issues to that upbringing. He had never married her mother due to those issues, but still wanted to be engaged in her life.

He truly seemed like a loving and caring father, fighting to get custody of her in order to provide her with a more stable home environment. Or at least, that's what he claimed.

I had to admire his persistence in wanting to care for his daughter and wasn't like so many fathers who just walked away from their kids. So despite these overwhelmingly alarming issues, I felt attracted to that seemingly nurturing and responsible side of him.

Plus, pastor mode kicked in. When I expressed my concerns about how I didn't feel equipped to deal with her and all of her problems, he pulled the, "but I think you'd be a good influence on her."

Appealing to my sense of vanity and desire to help all in one fell swoop. This guy was good.

Soon, conversations began turning toward longer-term plans. He had "retired" early from his job as a network administrator, so he was open to going anywhere and doing anything. He began suggesting he should move to Kearney to be near me. He even began looking for a job in Kearney.

I felt torn. Of course I wanted him closer; that would be more convenient. But that meant uprooting his now seventeen-year-old daughter. She'd finally gotten into the school she wanted to be at in Omaha, and here he was suggesting that he move to Kearney and uproot her from that.

The dilemma we faced as well: we both still wanted children. We were both thirty-eight. The window of opportunity there was rapidly disappearing. We'd be thirty-nine by the time she graduated from high school. Which meant even if we got married shortly after she graduated, I'd be forty by the time I could even conceivably be having a first child. With every year came increased risks and potential for problems.

In May, five months after our first date, he proposed at a wine and jazz festival in front of my senior pastor, friends, and parishioners. It wasn't a complete surprise; we'd been talking about marriage, obviously, just the time and date of the proposal was the unknown factor.

I suggested that we get married in October, but have him not move here yet in order to keep his daughter in the school she liked in Omaha. He immediately rejected that idea. No way was he going to be married and live apart from his wife. Little did I know there were other motives behind his rejecting this idea.

In June, he moved his daughter into my home, and he then went to stay with one of my parishioners until the wedding in October. As a pastor, you didn't live with someone, even if you were engaged.

It truly was the summer from hell. I thought maybe once he was actually living in the house with us things might get easier, but trying to be a mother who wasn't really her mother to a seventeen-year-old who was angry that she'd been moved away from her friends and school for her senior year was not going well.

More than once I nearly called off the wedding. More than once, he managed to talk me out of it, offering me reassurances and telling me things would be different once she was in school and we were actually married. More than once when I voiced my misgivings around parishioners, and suggested I might call the wedding off, they would get this horrified look on their face and go, "Oh, you don't mean that!"

The day before my wedding, I was having brunch with my matron of honor who had flown in from Indiana. (The seminary classmate whose friendship I bought with a cup of hot chocolate.) I was nervous and could barely eat.

ONCE UPON A NIGHTMARE

I admitted, I was scared. I chalked it up to the normal "cold feet" one gets when getting married.

I should have listened to my inner instincts that were screaming at me.

But my brain kept telling me—this was my last chance to have the fairy tale. This was the last chance to fulfill my dream.

On October 15, 2011, I married my not-so-Prince Charming.

And my dream, my fairy tale, rapidly became a nightmare.

Five

In a Mirror Dimly

"For now we see in a mirror, dimly, but then we will see face to face. Now I know only in part; then I will know fully, even as I have been fully known."

— 1 Corinthians 13:12

I KNOW THAT OUR life, our reality, is but a dim reflection of what God intends for our lives and our world. The pain, the sorrow, the suffering, and the poor self-image many of us carry around is a distorted reflection of what is intended. I always felt it was important to remember that the mirrors that existed in the Apostle Paul's day were typically polished metal of some sort. The image reflected back was not a clear, perfect replication. It was fuzzy and distorted.

I had no idea how quickly my life would become more than just the regular fuzzy and distorted. How quickly my life would turn me into someone I no longer recognized in the mirror, starting with a snorkeling trip while on my honeymoon.

Kicking my way to the bottom of the ocean floor, I could see the conch shell I wanted. It looked perfect and intact. My fingers closed around it, and I launched myself back toward the surface. As my head emerged from beneath the water, I could hear the sound of someone yelling for help.

My head swiveled around, searching for the source of the cry. I finally saw a man who was part of our snorkeling group. His legs had cramped up, and he was splashing around, trying desperately to keep his head above water. He wasn't wearing the small inflatable life jacket we'd been given, but then neither was I. I needed to dive to the bottom of the sea, and the life jacket wouldn't have allowed for that so I could hardly judge. Of course, I knew I was an excellent swimmer. I'm not sure this guy was.

I dropped the shell and let it sink forgotten back to the bottom of the sea as I swam toward his spluttering and thrashing form, clearly in distress as he continued to cry for help. Quickly closing the distance between us, my former training in lifesaving kicked in. It had been years since I'd used it, but some things you just never forget. I told him to relax and lean backwards. I promised, if he didn't flail around, I would not let his head go under water.

He complied, and I was able to successfully pull him back to the boat, where the guide finally realized what was going on and helped me get him aboard.

The man was much larger than me and despite the help of the buoyancy of the water, I was exhausted having dragged him across the ocean. Admittedly, I also was not in the best shape due to my bulging cervical discs that had made exercising tricky.

I collapsed down on the seat, ready to be done for the day. My husband was still out in the water. He'd apparently witnessed my rescue operation. I smiled at him as he climbed into the boat.

He glared at me. Clearly annoyed and disgruntled. No words of affirmation. No congratulations. No even asking if I was okay after I'd just dragged a man nearly twice my size through the water and was clearly spent.

He held up his foot which had a little puncture mark and said, "I was injured, but you didn't come save me."

My mouth dropped open, and I stared at him in astonishment as I said, "I didn't know you needed saving."

A girl spends her whole life dreaming about how wonderfully romantic her honeymoon is going to be. We'd traveled to the exotic islands of St. Lucia and St. Vincent's, where I'd managed to fall part way down a volcano and reinjure my neck that was already plagued by those bulging cervical discs. No one to blame for that misery but myself.

Still, there had been the restaurant on St. Vincent's he had wanted to go to that we wound up walking nearly two miles to get to in my flip flops. My feet were covered in blisters by the time we got back to the hotel. I tried to not be angry. I didn't want to be angry on my honeymoon. Yet, I was angry that he hadn't figured out a way to get us a ride to and from the restaurant. It was with these blistered feet and painful back and shoulder that I had saved a man from drowning, which resulted in incurring the resentment of my husband.

I did not even know how to respond. Why was I suddenly feeling guilty, as though I hadn't been paying enough attention to him? The sea had always been my happy place. The thrumming quiet of the ocean sounds beneath the water were always so soothing. Yes, I'd kind of wandered off on my own in search of the perfect conch shell I wanted to take home. The one I'd been forced to drop was the second one I'd lost that day. The first I lost when I handed it to the guide in the boat. A crab apparently came out and bit his finger, and he wound up dropping the shell. The water just under the boat was too deep for me to dive that far.

As I sat there breathing heavily, trying to recover from just saving a man's life—and having now lost the two shells I'd found—I was feeling like I had somehow failed my husband because I was off doing my thing and wasn't paying attention to his apparent need.

I asked to see his foot. There was indeed a small puncture wound that had some purple discoloration to it, but it wasn't swelling and didn't look too bad. I told him we'd get it checked out when we got back to shore. He crossed his arms and sat back, not looking at me.

I set my jaw and grew equally angry. How on earth was he mad at me over this?

Suffice it to say, the honeymoon was over before it was even literally over. By the time we got home, I had begun to have serious fears I'd made a terrible mistake.

No Princess had to deal with her Prince being upset that she'd saved someone else's life. Weren't they supposed to be proud of their wives?

The next few months were not any easier. We spent most of our time dealing with his daughter. I daily would get a phone call from the school nurse that she was sick, or not feeling well, or had fainted. The fainting was a real problem, but we'd been taking her to cardiologists, neurologists, everyone to try and figure out what could be causing them. They continually turned up nothing, and I began wondering if her issues weren't simply psychosomatic. Her father blamed it on the HPV vaccine, claiming the problems didn't start until then. (Years later I would find out she needed a pacemaker as her heart kept stopping. Why the cardiologist at the time didn't pick up on the problem, I have no idea.)

The emergency bills continued to mount. Despite insurance, it was several hundred dollars every time someone called 911, and she wound up in the ER almost weekly. Even while we'd been on our honeymoon, we received word she'd fainted and landed in the hospital. Part of me began to think she was doing it just to get attention. We repeatedly caught her in lies, and she would, at almost every opportunity, defy her father's wishes and orders.

I was constantly being caught in the middle as she'd come to me wanting me to reason with him. I easily realized this as a manipulation. The problem was, I didn't know how to really stop the manipulation. I put all three of us into therapy, hoping that would help with some of the issues. I hoped I would learn some techniques to not be triangulated constantly.

I kept telling myself, repeatedly, that it would eventually get better. When she moved out of the house, things would settle down. I could endure anything I needed to; there would eventually be an end.

Shortly after she turned eighteen, his daughter moved out of the house following an argument over whether or not she could leave the house at midnight to go spend time with three guys. I had to side with her father on this one—that was not okay or appropriate at midnight. He threatened that if she left the house that night, never to come back.

She left.

The next day, he changed the locks on the house.

It was embarrassing to have the school call me and plead with me that an eighteen-year-old couldn't be homeless and couch surfing. I didn't know what to do. She wasn't my child. I had very little say over her life. She was impossible to deal with. She defied her father at every turn. I was in over my head and had no idea how to deal with these realities.

True, it was my home ultimately. It was in my name, and I could decide whether I wanted her in my home or not. But relationships are far more complicated than who simply owns the deed to the house you're living in.

And that relationship was about to get even more complicated.

We were only into month seven of our marriage when I was sitting in my office with our media director, and I received the following text from my husband:

"I'm in jail."

I laughed at first.

I thought it was a joke.

It had to be a joke.

It was, in fact, not a joke.

I called him, confused, and he quickly rattled off the following instructions as they were going to take his phone away.

"I've been arrested. I'm in the Buffalo County jail but they're going to move me and take my phone. Come get all my stuff."

Then the line went dead.

To say I was flabbergasted and confused would be an understatement. I had no idea what was happening. I sat there, staring at my phone, then looked across my desk at my media director, who was staring at me wide-eyed. I finally just went, "He's apparently really in jail."

My voice and hands were shaking as I still was not comprehending this reality. I quickly gathered my things together and made my way, somehow, to my car.

I arrived at the Buffalo County jail to pick up his phone and other personal effects. They couldn't tell me where he was at this point as when the Marshals move you, they don't tell anyone where they're headed. All I knew was he had been arrested by twelve U.S. Marshals at his place of employment and was going to be in Federal Court in Omaha in forty-eight hours. He likely had been moved to Lexington, as it was the nearest Federal holding facility, but I didn't know for sure.

I called my parents, bawling. What was I supposed to do? They were as dumbfounded and shocked as I was. I tried calling an attorney he had mentioned he had used in the past, but that guy was going to cost thousands and thousands of dollars I didn't have to defend a Federal case. Eventually I did get a call from a court-appointed attorney, who at least was able to tell me his court date would be in Omaha a few days later. At that point, I grabbed George, our brand new Cavalier King Charles Spaniel puppy we had just picked up from a breeder two weeks earlier, and headed to my parents.

Nothing prepares you for a jolt to the system like this. No one warns you about what happens when Prince Charming turns into the villain of the story.

The next few weeks were a haze of confusion and disorientation. What had he done? Why was this happening? I felt as though my entire world was falling apart. I broke down and cried non-stop. I was confused. Lost. How did I explain to the senior pastor I worked with that I had to leave town suddenly because my husband had just been arrested by Federal Marshals and I had no idea why?

All I managed to glean was this had something to do with some trouble he'd gotten into a few years earlier regarding the mortgage company that was in the process of foreclosing on his house. Something about "intimidating" a federal employee at the HUD offices. A rather minor, misdemeanor offense—or so I was led to believe.

The next few days were a whirlwind that I scarcely remember. I was never told what had happened or what he'd done exactly. Everything just seemed like it was surreal, and multiple times a day I kept asking, "How is this my life?"

My mom and I arrived at that first hearing in Omaha a little early. We sat down in the courtroom as the judge was hearing the case of a third probation violation for a drug charge. The judge simply extended his probation period and let him go.

I had some hope. This judge seemed lenient and reasonable. I mean, it wasn't like my husband had violated his probation multiple times, right?

As the U.S. Marshals brought him into the courtroom, the judge's demeanor immediately changed. He became tense and angry. He questioned whether my husband was even mentally competent.

I mean...what? A judge was questioning my husband's sanity? What on earth was going on?

I would not get any answers that day, though the judge did remove himself from the case, saying he could no longer be the judge in the case as he was not unbiased based on my husband's threats to him and his staff.

Again...*what?!*

Who were they talking about? What were they talking about? Threats to a federal judge? That was insane.

His court-appointed attorney gave me a sympathetic look and simply stated, "You've never stepped foot in a courtroom before, have you?"

I shook my head, still utterly befuddled at what was going on. I mean that wasn't entirely true. I'd sat on a jury once in Los Angeles for a civil case awarding damages to an accident victim, but aside from that, no. I'd never been in a court room for personal reasons.

After the attorney walked out, one of the Marshals walked up to me and again gave me another of those sympathetic looks. "If you want to see him, he will be at the Douglas County Jail tomorrow after five. You can visit him then."

On the way home, I received a phone call from him. He was giving me "permission" to divorce him. Anyone else probably would have taken him up on it. I should have at that juncture. I was in such a state of confusion, however, that I simply said we'd discuss it later.

I learned more about the Department of Corrections than I ever cared to that week. If you wanted to receive phone calls, you needed to put money into a phone account for them to call out on. You had to put money in their account to buy additional food from the commissary. When you did visit, you didn't get to see them in person—you got to see them on a video screen with a phone you talked through. They had a strict dress code for visitors. I walked in wearing shorts and was informed that they would not allow me in to talk to him if I was wearing those shorts. Being an hour from Lincoln, I had a momentary panic attack—what could I wear? Luckily, for some reason, I had some of my step-daughter's clothes in the car and I was able to slide into some of her yoga pants which were apparently considered acceptable attire compared to the shorts. How I fit into those pants I have no idea given his eighteen-year-old daughter was easily eight sizes smaller than me. But they were passable, and I got to see him and talk to him through the video phone.

I also determined after that visit I wasn't going to bother coming back. I could talk to him on the phone from home; I didn't need to drive to Omaha to do that nonsense.

In the meantime, my brother was in the hospital having a problem with a dissecting aorta so my mother left to go to Minneapolis while my father and I stayed back.

A week later, my father and I sat in on the hearing with the new judge and still didn't get a lot of answers. Now I was not exactly the most lucid and aware during these hearings. I was such an emotional wreck, my father had given me Klonopin to calm me down, and I wasn't paying close attention to certain details. My father and mother would both later tell me that when he walked into the courtroom and saw them with me, he would glare at them, clearly angry that they were there to witness this. At one point, he apparently even pointed at my mother and shook his head at her, as if to say, "I don't want you here."

The prosecuting attorney walked in with a large CD player and a stack of files under his arm. I was curious: what on earth was he going to be playing in court?

I never found out. My husband quickly accepted a plea deal and was sentenced to house arrest for the next four months on top of five years of probation. Due to the plea deal, I was not privy to whatever the actual charges or problems were, nor what was on the recordings the prosecutor was going to play. All his probation officer would tell me about what he'd done was that "it was bad."

I came back later that evening to pick him up after he'd been released and we drove back to Kearney. I angrily said, "You're never doing this again, or we're done."

He of course swore that he would never land himself in jail again.

Unfortunately, he would not abide by that promise.

The next four months were a haze. House arrest involved wearing an ankle monitor and having to request permission to literally go to dinner, grocery shopping, church—basically any sort of trip outside of going to and from work.

He struggled to follow the rules. He constantly battled with his probation officer, claiming they were violating his rights or some such thing. He seemed to forget—probation meant he no longer had the same rights as everyone else. Whenever I pointed this out to him, he'd vehemently argue that yes, he did!

He'd also been assigned a new probation officer. His previous one had been a woman, and they determined he was too dangerous to continue under her supervision so they switched him to what I would call your much more "stereotypical" type of probation office. A stocky, bald man built like a bouncer.

They wanted to monitor his computer usage, which seemed really strange to me.

We began fighting a lot, mainly over how he was dealing with the whole house arrest thing. I've always been the type of person to play by the rules, to essentially do what I'm told. His constant struggling and pushing the boundaries of what was allowed baffled me.

Once he came home, I started demanding some answers about what had happened.

I was shown emails, court documents, all relating to what he had allegedly done. None of it seemed that bad, and I was confused as to why he was being treated so harshly. It simply didn't make sense!

Based on what he had presented to me as his evidence, his mortgage company had been ripping him off. He had the documentation to show all the payments, all the correspondence between them. Their refusal to work with him on payment plans when he'd lost his job at the Marriott—a job he claimed to have lost due to downsizing after September 11th. (That was a lie, but I didn't know it at the time.)

He had contacted HUD asking, or rather demanding, they investigate his mortgage company for fraud. When they refused to do so, he lost his temper with them and screamed and yelled at the HUD officer.

He was charged then with intimidating a federal officer. A misdemeanor offense that resulted in five years of probation.

So what on earth was this whole Federal Marshals arresting him and holding him without bail for a week all about?

Well, it all went back to when my mother and I were making plans to go up and be with my brother because of his dissecting aorta, and we didn't know whether he was going to live yet or not.

Apparently, my husband had a court date that following Monday I was unaware of—for violating his probation related to the intimidation charge. He'd been refusing to turn in the paperwork to set up the computer monitoring, so he was being taken back to court for violating the terms of his probation.

When he found out about my brother, he played the dutiful husband and offered to go with me. I told him there was no need. I wasn't even sure yet if I was going to go.

He ignored me, and apparently called the judge's office, demanding his court date be rescheduled. When they refused, he began to threaten them and said that someone would be leaving court in a body bag. (That was what the prosecuting attorney was going to play in court.) That triggered the judge issuing an arrest warrant determining the body bag comment was yet another threat and added it to the list of charges.

The version of this I got was that he had tried to get his court date changed so he could come with me, but they were refusing, and kept hanging up on him. His request made them afraid that he wouldn't show up, and that's why they sent the Marshals to arrest him.

To add to all of this, my bought-with-hot-chocolate best friend from seminary's senior pastor killed himself two weeks after my husband came home. I couldn't go to the funeral in Indiana to help support her, but a few weeks later I was at least able to fly out and help her with their vacation bible school. We were both emotional wrecks trying to navigate our own very raw traumatic experiences.

Meanwhile, I eventually saw a copy of the court-ordered psychological evaluation they'd done on my husband to determine his sanity. He'd been diagnosed with a slew of different personality disorders, the two that stood out being narcissistic and histrionic. Personality disorders didn't qualify as insanity and incompetent to stand trial, however.

I had zero comprehension of what that meant. We didn't cover personality disorders during seminary. The analysis recommended anger management and that I, as his wife, could be instrumental in helping him with his therapy. So, of course, I figured therapy would help and wanted to do whatever I could to help him with that.

I struggled to make sense of a life and relationship that had been spiraling for the first year into a chasm of chaos that seemed more like a Lifetime movie script than real life. I lived in a fog, clinging to the hope that the crazy around me would at some point settle down and "normal" would one day return. I awoke every morning taking a deep breath, forcing myself to get out of bed, then would take a long look in the mirror and wonder where the vibrant woman I had once been had gone.

I was taking Ambien like it was candy every night to sleep.

"It will get better," I told myself every single morning as the reflection in the mirror became more and more foreign to me. I kept telling myself that there would come a time when every day wouldn't be a battle that chips away just a little more of your soul. Someday, you won't feel the despondency and sense of swimming upstream. Someday, you'll wake up, look in the mirror, and won't have yet another wound slicing open another piece of your spirit.

Someday, the crazy will end.

That became my mantra, even though eventually the image in the mirror became a complete and utter stranger.

There were bags under my eyes, I rarely smiled, my eyes had dulled and lost their spark. I never messed with my hair beyond pulling it back into a ponytail and had long since abandoned wearing make-up. My brow had become permanently pinched with stress, and I'd gotten considerably heavier. Part of that was due to the fact that despite every attempt I made at losing weight, my husband would practically force food down me when I'd shove the plate away saying I'd had enough. Even my mother had noticed this tendency and frequently commented, "It's almost like he wants you gain weight the way he shoves food at you all the time."

I felt like Hansel in Hansel and Gretel where the wicked witch kept him in a cage and was fattening him up so she could eat him later on.

This was not my life. It couldn't be. I didn't recognize myself anymore—a shell of the person I had once been; spiritually, emotionally and mentally beaten down into a world where simply surviving had become my goal. Nothing made sense, and I was torn between my sense of duty and saving my own sanity. Admitting that even otherwise intelligent people sometimes make really bad choices in life was not easy. Tears were the daily norm, and my reality had become so skewed that there were no longer any lines between truth and fiction. It all melded together into some surreal fantasy-like world where everything had been turned upside down.

We even argued about the dog he had talked me into getting. I hadn't wanted a dog initially. Not because I didn't like them—I'd been raised with Brittany and Springer Spaniels—but because I was used to being single and not being home enough to take care of them properly. He finally wore me down shortly before he was arrested, and we got George. We fought because my husband was mad that the dog had bonded with me rather than him. Going to jail for a week right after getting the dog would do that. So he wanted another one, one that he could bond with.

I put my foot down on that one and said absolutely not. The last thing I needed in my life was another element of chaos.

Life had become fuzzy and distorted.

My fuzzy, distorted life was not only *not* what I had ever hoped and imagined my life and my marriage would be, it had become a waking nightmare. Not just a dim reflection of what was intended—but a twisted distortion of everything I'd ever hoped and dreamed as my world came shattering down around me.

Six
Sighs Too Deep for Words

> *"Likewise the Spirit helps us in our weakness; for we do not know how to pray as we ought, but that the very Spirit intercedes with sighs too deep for words."*
>
> — Romans 8:26

MY HOPE FOR A fairy tale life had collapsed around me. There was nothing magical or even romantic left in my world. Just survival. The written word eluded me; which, as a writer, was devastating. When I had no way to describe the emotions that were flooding through me like a rushing torrent of pain, confusion, and grief, I always felt Romans 8 captured that feeling all too well. When words failed. When all I had were deep sighs and groans, the spirit had to intercede on my behalf, groaning and sighing along with me. For me. Alongside me.

Sometimes I did attempt words, but they failed me during this time in ways that art did not. So I took what words I did manage to eek out on paper, and I plastered them to a piece of canvas board and began painting my lament, covering up the pages that contained these words:

REBECCA J. CRAIG

I cry out to the Lord night and day.
Take this pain, take this sorrow.
Wipe the tears away.
Make me content,
that your love and grace are sufficient.
I crawl inside myself,
trying to shut out the world.
Trying to recognize that what other people
have is not the life for me.
That our world is hurting and in pain,
so why should I be any different?
There are no words to describe the pain,
the sorrow, the betrayal, the confusion.

ONCE UPON A NIGHTMARE

It simply is.
Emotional pain and stress is invisible.
It hurts the soul.
It is the silent torture day in and day out.
Not knowing how your life became a living nightmare.
Daily I wake, focused on simply breathing,
putting one one foot in front of the other.
To have thought you loved and were loved in return by another,
only to find out it was all a sham.
A joke.
You were simply a target in a sick and twisted game.
Grief runs deep within the soul.
The spirit is shattered.

When I'm under extreme emotional distress and pain, I try to write poetry. I emphasize try. Poetry has never been my gift. I want things to rhyme. I don't care about iambic pentameter, haikus, or all the other ways in which poetry can be expressed. For me, it's gotta rhyme. It has to have a rhythm that can be sung like lyrics. So this is what came out and then found itself forever secured to the canvas by the strokes of a paintbrush.

Tears and tears, my tears they fall.
Unabated they do flow.
Why does no one hear my call?
Only God can know.

The darkness it creeps and consumes my soul.
My life has sunk so low.
What purpose serves this gaping hole?
Only God can know.

I scream, I yell, to no avail.
No one hears my soul.
Why, oh why, must I follow this trail?
Only God can know.

What terrible deed did I commit within?
Why make me love him so?
Am I being punished for some unknown sin?
Only God can know.

Have I not paid the price?
Been tortured enough by love?
Or is it truly just a roll of the dice?
Only God can know.

They say "do not question your trials of woe,
God has more important tasks."
But if only God can know,
Who else am I to ask?

    Who else am I to ask indeed. I was grateful for the Spirit that intercedes, because there were times when the words I wanted to say to God were not reverent and filled with awe.
    They were filled with lament and anger. Admittedly I know my poetry reveals bad theology. I don't truly believe I'm being punished...or do I?
    You may know in your head what good theology is. What you believe about the nature of God.
    That doesn't help how you actually *feel* about God at times, however. I frequently felt that I must have done something at some point to deserve this heartache, to be denied my dreams, to be denied my heart's desire. That in my stubborn insistence that I fulfill my childhood dream, my husband was sent to me to prove a point and teach me a lesson.

That I am supposed to be alone. Do not tread down this path again. I told you—I have other plans for you.

Again. This is not good theology, and I would absolutely tell anyone else who was feeling this way to stop it right now; those thoughts are not from God. Those thoughts are not representative of God. God is not that petty or that vindictive.

Yet, one cannot help how one feels. Probably why I decided I needed to destroy those thoughts within my painting. Yet, my lament lives on. My grief continues.

With sighs too deep for words.

It was with those heavy sighs that I would find myself almost exactly two and a half years after I walked down the aisle, facing one of the most difficult decisions of my life in terms of my marriage.

It was morning.

I lay in bed feeling an understandable sense of dread. My husband got up and headed to the bathroom for his morning half-hour constitutional on the toilet. I didn't stir and pretended I was asleep, trying to keep my breathing even and rhythmic. He probably knew I wasn't asleep. I'm a light sleeper. Everything wakes me up.

He finally returned to the room and changed into his clothes for the day. He seemed content to also pretend that I was asleep until he was ready to leave. Then he leaned over, kissed me goodbye, and told me he'd call me later.

I grunted a response and rolled over on my other side.

I continued to lie there with my eyes shut until I heard his car leave the driveway. I let out a heavy sigh of relief and rolled over on my back to stare at the ceiling, relishing the quiet. There was only the sound of the dog snoring in his kennel in the kitchen. I was grateful he didn't wake the dog up.

It was hard to breathe, though every morning was like that. For two years I'd felt this heavy, oppressive weight that just sat on my chest, threatening to suffocate me.

My cell phone rang.

Somehow, I knew what was to come as I glanced at the caller ID. It was my husband.

My heart rate began to quicken, my anxiety suddenly spiking. With a sense of trepidation and even some hesitation, I slid the keypad toward the green phone symbol to answer it.

"U.S. Marshals are on the way to arrest me."

My breath caught, my heart stopped. Though I had to admit the statement did not completely catch me by surprise. Not this time.

I had been expecting this.

"You need to come and pick up my wallet and stuff. It will be in my car."

"How do you know they're coming?" I asked, surprised at how calm I both felt and sounded compared to the last time I received a call like this from him.

"They went to the north office first," he explained. "I got a call warning me. I'm just going to sit in the parking lot and wait."

Ah.

I breathed a sigh of relief. Relief!

The night before he sent out to several friends and family what I could only refer to as his "manifesto" that he titled, "Murdered by my Government." In it he'd outlined all the problems he'd had with his mortgage company, his ensuing legal troubles, and stating that the federal prosecutor was trying to have him killed. It was nine pages worth of crazy that would ultimately cause even his best friend of nine years to cut ties with him.

Strangely, while others were in disbelief over the nine pages of insanity, I was feeling relief that at least he was not going to fight and resist arrest like he'd been threatening to do since he walked away from the Residential Re-entry Center (RRC) that previous Saturday that he'd been sentenced to. That I wasn't going to have to watch my husband get shot to death in my front yard. I don't know if I could have handled that.

I still remember the moment of disbelief followed by horror as he came walking through the door on Saturday as my parents and I had just sat down for dinner.

A few months earlier, following an altercation with his daughter where the police were called, he was brought up on a second probation violation.

After she moved out of the house and graduated, she moved in with some guy out near Fremont, Nebraska, where her grandparents lived. In a not at all stunning turn of events, I received a phone call from the mother of the young man she was living with who let us know that she was now pregnant.

A few days later we met her and her boyfriend at a local restaurant to talk about it. I don't recall what exactly transpired during that conversation but whatever happened, her father became angry and stormed out of the restaurant. We returned home, and she and her boyfriend followed. She ran toward the house to try to get in before he closed the door and managed to stick her foot in the doorway, stopping the door from closing. I don't honestly know what happened next. All I know is he eventually got the door shut, and then he called the police, wanting her removed from the property.

Meanwhile, she called the police as well, claiming he'd shoved her down the stairs of the front porch. I didn't see that happen and wasn't sure how that was even possible given he never came out from behind the door he was trying to slam shut on her.

Regardless of what the truth was, the police officer wrote him up on an assault charge—thus violating his probation.

I was desperate at this point and began calling in whatever pull I had with people, trying to find an attorney that could make that charge go away. It was bogus in my view. Yes, they were arguing, but he hadn't laid a hand on her from what I'd seen. If she fell off those steps, it was not because he threw her down them.

We eventually succeeded in getting the case dropped, but the damage was done in terms of his probation violation. Despite the charges being dropped, he was still in violation and thus had to go to court a second time.

That resulted in his being sentenced to the RRC, which is essentially a type of half-way house, for possibly up to six months. He would be able to go to work, but he'd have to live at this facility and be monitored whenever he wasn't at work.

He utilized the excuse of his work making him travel for the next four months to delay checking into the RRC. Eventually, after spending two months in Atlanta, and another two months in Dallas, he was ordered by the judge to stop delaying and report to the facility or the Federal Marshals would once again come for him.

It was Holy Week, which for a pastor is one of our busiest, most exhausting times of the year. He assisted us at the church with our Good Friday service, and then Saturday morning was set to report to the facility. My parents, not wanting me to spend Easter alone under the circumstances, came out to visit.

We were sitting outside on my deck Saturday evening eating a nice dinner when I suddenly heard the front door open, and in waltzed my husband. Our jaws collectively dropped as he strolled out onto the deck. I didn't even pretend to hide my shock and anger.

"What are you doing here?" I demanded.

He shrugged. "They weren't going to allow me to go to work until I did their orientation, and their orientation wasn't going to be until Wednesday. That didn't work for me. So I left."

I sat there in utter shock, spluttering my words at this point. "What do you mean it wouldn't work for you? You…you can't just *walk away* from a court ordered RRC facility!" I said in a strained, tense voice.

Again, he shrugged and walked back into the house.

My parents and I just sat there and stared at one another, dumbfounded. What on earth was he thinking? He had to know they were going to arrest him, right? He had to know this time, they were going to send him to jail. This would be a third probation violation. There was no way the judge was going to go lenient again.

I was exhausted for our Easter services the next morning. Exhausted, angry, and anxious. For all I knew, the U.S. Marshals might storm the church. On Easter. Or be waiting out in the parking lot.

Imagine spending Easter morning as a pastor worrying about federal marshals storming your church. That was my life.

Every night after that he would sit on the edge of the bed with the blinds open, looking for police lights, knowing they would likely come and arrest him.

They finally came. But not to our home.

Not to *my* home, I quickly corrected myself. He didn't own it. His name wasn't even attached to it. I jolted a little at this mental correction. I'd already begun to go through the process of listing my assets in my head.

Why was I doing this?

I knew why I was doing it. I'd warned him what would happen if he was ever sent to jail again.

I quickly shoved that thought aside.

"Okay," I said again, and hung up the phone. I sat up in bed and looked around the cluttered bedroom. I'd quit caring about keeping things tidy.

I should have been crying. I should have been upset.

But I just felt...numb. Resigned.

Oddly, I didn't even feel rushed. In fact, I laid back down for a little while and just stared at the ceiling some more. Why didn't I feel the sense of confusion, the utter sense of despair I did the first time this happened? Had I really become so used to the idea that being told U.S. Marshals might come knocking on my door that the prospect didn't even phase me anymore?

I lay there for a while longer before eventually dragging myself out of bed. I realized it was Wednesday, which meant I would see the therapist that afternoon.

The marriage counselor that I'd practically had to threaten him with divorce to go to with me.

I got ready for work much the same way I did every day. Let the dog out, fed him and re-kenneled him.

Only this day I had a stop to make before going to the office.

I called a friend and colleague in ministry and asked him to drive me over to the south office so I could pick up my husband's car and personal items. Somehow, I was able to tell him that my husband had once again been arrested and not break down. It really is a mystery to me how this was even possible.

He gave me that all too-familiar sympathetic look. He had done our pre-marital counseling. I admit, I felt a twinge of anger regarding that. There had to have been red flags in that pre-marital test we took, right? I remember the results had said something about how my husband suffered from an extremely poor self-image. I noted at the time that seemed strange, as lacking self-confidence was not one of the things I would have pegged. But I didn't really know what to do with that information. In hindsight, it makes more sense. Never marry someone who scores under a thirty percent on self-confidence. They will make up for that internal lack of self-confidence by over-compensating externally.

I got in my friend's car, and he took me to my husband's office in near silence.

Sometimes silence is better.

Some pastors know this. We call it the "ministry of presence."

He knew this.

Trying not to draw any attention to myself, I quietly slipped into the driver's seat of my husband's light blue Pacifica that was parked just outside the front of his workplace. The center console contained his wallet, phone, wedding ring and silver cross necklace. I picked up the wedding ring and stared at it for a long moment before dropping it back down in the console.

Settling into the seat, I clenched the steering wheel tightly and took a deep breath.

I knew there was no point in trying to get a hold of him in the next twenty-four hours. Been down this road before.

I drove back to my house and walked inside with his things. For a moment, I just stood inside the door, staring at them in my hands. The phone, the wallet, the necklace...the wedding ring.

Feeling a wave of rage wash over me, I dropped everything but the ring. I stared at it a moment before gripping it tightly and then with a deep, guttural scream, I launched it toward the wall, where it bounced harmlessly and relatively noiselessly off the drywall and onto the hardwood floor. The scream awakened our dog, George, who'd been snoring loudly in his kennel in the kitchen. Seeing me, he stood up and began to paw at the door to let him out.

I obliged, and I sat on floor and allowed him to crawl into my lap as he shoved his nose in my face and began snorting his little pig-snorts at me. I finally began to sob and could not stop even as I got ready to leave for the therapy appointment.

ONCE UPON A NIGHTMARE

I had no words. There was a profound depth to my desires and longings that transcended ordinary language that resonated only with the realm of the extraordinary. Only those sobs...that were too deep for words.

Seven
Shattered

> *"My soul is in deep anguish. How long, Lord, how long?"*
>
> — Psalm 6:3

WE SUFFER LOSS IN a multitude of ways. We lose loved ones through death, divorce, accidents, illnesses, and broken relationships. Loss of a job, a meaningful career, facing an illness of our own or a changed way of life; no matter what the cause, you know what it's like to feel as though everything around you is falling apart and shattering. Shattered lives. Shattered love. Shattered trust. Shattered dreams. Even your very being—shattered.

Broken lives are a part of the human experience. We all have times and moments where we feel as though a sledgehammer has slammed into the fragile case we keep around our lives and our hearts, shattering everything to its very core. What we thought of as authentic and true now becomes cracked and skewed; everything has an edge, and everything is seen through reflecting shards that twist and distort what we once thought was tangible and genuine. There is nothing more devastating and shattering than having your entire reality, everything you thought to be normal about life or about a person, falling apart in a shower of tinkling glass. Your hopes and dreams for a particular future—shattered.

It does amaze me how fragile the lives we live tend to be at times, and how quickly everything can change and fall apart around us. Even faith is changed in some way when such life-altering events occur. Not that one necessarily loses it—I would have been lost without my faith and the faith community—but my faith had changed. My relationship and understanding of God changed as a result of such events. Whether that's good or bad I think is not the right way to look at it—but simply that it is. Our faith changes throughout life, our outlooks change based on events and experiences we go through. A broken and shattered cross is endemic of what the cross itself stands for—a broken and shattered humanity that strung God up on a cross when he dared get too close to us.

Trust between humanity and God has long been shattered. Trust between individuals also has shattered. Some events even cause us to finally, and at last, question trust in ourselves, shattering our illusions that we always know what's best for us or thinking we somehow have some type of control in this world and of those around us. All of that is shattered.

"Shattered" is the world we live in.

Shattered was the world I was trying to navigate as I realized my life was swirling down the toilet.

The day I had to file for divorce, I was a puddle. There's no traditional fairy tale that deals with this issue. The Princess divorcing Prince Not-So-Charming.

I distinctly remember sitting in my attorney's office for that first time as she calmly asked me why I wanted a divorce.

My next words would be effectively slamming the door on the primary dream I had held my entire life. I was walking away from my husband. I was walking away from the hope and dream of children. My lifelong desire to raise a family was evaporating before my very eyes.

My long-held dreams were shattering. The fairy tale had gone up in smoke. My once dreamed-of Prince Charming was now nothing more than a pile of broken promises all around me. This was yet one more dream that was being added to the list of dreams I'd walked away from.

I grieved this at a deep level. The worst part was, despite knowing I needed to get a divorce, I still loved my husband.

I did not want a divorce.

I *needed* a divorce.

If I had any hope of surviving and thriving in life, I needed to divorce the man I still loved. He was killing me, slowly. Not physically, but spiritually, emotionally, and mentally. He was killing my soul, he was killing my spirit; he was crushing my sanity.

Even from jail he was able to reach out and wreak havoc when he called.

"They're trying to kill me!" came the frantic voice of my husband on the other end of the phone. It crackled with static in that way landline phones do where the connection isn't always the best at times, and, oh yeah, when it's also being monitored by the Department of Corrections.

"What?" I asked, figuring I hadn't heard him right.

"They're trying to kill me with food! They're ignoring my gluten and dairy allergy!"

"Your what?" I said again, incredulity filling my voice, as I glanced into the kitchen of my parents' home. Earlier that day we'd been in court, where he once again was trying to reach some kind of plea agreement for violating his probation for the third time. My hand began to shake, as it had begun to do quite frequently in those days. I bit my tongue, refraining from saying more, knowing that the line was being monitored. I should have probably called him out, exposed him right there as a liar and a fraud. Instead, I sucked in my breath and held it until I started to feel dizzy.

What I wanted to ask—no, rather, what I wanted to shout through the phone was, "What the hell are you talking about?! I've lived with you for nearly three years and not once has the issue of a gluten or dairy allergy ever come up!" With all the pizza, milk products, and bread we had eaten over the years, a gluten or dairy allergy certainly would have come to light before this particular day.

"My gluten and dairy allergy!" he continued to insist. "We'll discuss it later."

Much later, I thought, as he continued to complain about the accommodations and how he was being treated by the Douglas County Jail system.

"My mattress is terrible. I've got a bruise on my hip where the springs are poking through."

"Oh. I'm sorry." What else was I supposed to say? Sorry babe, really sucks that you don't have luxury hotel accommodations being provided for you while you are under the care of the U.S. Government's penal system, but then, they're not exactly known for splurging on extravagances even when you aren't being held in custody. Just sayin'.

More idle complaints droned on in my ear until the mechanized female voice informed us we only had sixty seconds left on the call. He wrapped it up with a barrage of "I love yous" before the mechanized voice returned to tell me the call had ended.

My trembling fingers pressed the red circular phone icon on my smartphone and hung up. The screen went dark, and I was left sitting in silence.

He's gone insane, I thought. No, really and truly insane this time.

This time.

That shouldn't have been a qualifier, but it was. It was the second time I'd had to navigate my way around how the phone system worked with the

Department of Corrections. The second time I'd had to figure out how to get online and put money in his account so he could call me without having to make it a collect call every time.

I took a deep breath across from the attorney, the question of why I wanted a divorce still lingered as the conversation from the morning before with the marriage counselor we had seen just once still bouncing around in my head.

"You do realize you're married to a sociopath, right?"

Sociopath.

Nope, hadn't made that connection quite yet, doc, but now that you have done that for me—how far and fast can I run?

Well, Narcissistic Personality Disorder (NPD) to be exact. But those words I had read on his psychological evaluation two years earlier had not set off the alarm bells. They should have—combined with histrionic and obsessive-compulsive personality disorders. He had a fun cocktail of Axis II Cluster B disorders.

Which at the time, meant absolutely nothing to me.

An NPD diagnosis just meant he was a bit self-centered and sometimes had delusions at grandeur, right? I mean, I knew he didn't always operate in the realm of reality, but...pathological? He could get therapy and work through the problems, right? He was going to court-ordered anger management counseling. All of that would work if he wanted it to—right? All his problems stemmed from one primary issue in his life, and if we could just put that behind us, things would get better—right?

Wrong.

My response was shock. "Well," I finally managed to squeak out, "I know he was diagnosed with a narcissistic personality disorder."

She shrugged. "It's a spectrum and sliding scale of sociopathy."

Sociopathy.

The word hung in the air.

My husband...was a sociopath.

The connection slammed into place. Narcissism and sociopathy were so closely related they were difficult to distinguish without a full mental health examination.

A full mental health examination he'd had, and they hadn't pegged him with an anti-social personality disorder, but I suppose that "sliding scale" she spoke of meant that it was likely mixed in there as well along with the histrionic, narcissistic and obsessive compulsive personality disorders.

In that moment, I knew I could not 'fix' my husband. I knew no amount of therapy was going to make him better. I knew I could not save or stay in this marriage.

For the past two years I had endured his house arrest and two, going on a third, probation violation hearings. I'd watched myself become a mere shadow of who I'd once been. All in the hopes that one day, this chaos, these legal issues, would be over and done with.

In that moment, I knew that would never be my reality. That it would only get worse, not better. That my fairy tale dream was dead, and all that remained was the ongoing nightmare that I was never going to escape from if I continued to stay with him.

His legal problems were never going away. He would never allow them to go away. He wasn't capable of it. He wasn't capable of living within the normal constraints of society. He couldn't handle being told what to do. Having people control his life in any fashion.

This was never going to end.

In that moment, I felt both horrified and relieved. Horrified because I'd failed to connect those dots and did not pick up on them earlier.

Relieved, because at least that meant I wasn't going crazy, and I wasn't the one being unreasonable like he tried to have me believe.

When I finished with my therapy session, I walked in a haze of tears across the street to my colleague in ministry who I had spoken with on several occasions over the past two years about everything going on with my marriage and his legal troubles. We sat down. He sighed deeply and gave me this analogy:

"Imagine there's a driver of a nuclear waste truck that crashes. The driver is dead. You witness this and feel like you should rush in and see if you can save him. The reality is, if you try to save him, you only wind up dead yourself. So you have a choice: there can be two casualties in your marriage—or one. You can save yourself, but you cannot save him." He then prodded me to consider what my next step needed to be.

I reluctantly stated: "I need to find an attorney."

So here I now sat, across from the attorney, her dark eyes boring into mine wanting to know why I was sitting in her office requesting to file for divorce.

I took a deep, shuddering breath and answered: "Because he's crazy. He's sitting in federal prison. And I just can't do this anymore." I then burst into tears and had no idea what we talked about for the rest of the meeting as I cried the whole time. I think she finally realized that I was pretty useless at this point and scheduled another meeting to discuss the particulars.

I went home, curled up on the floor, and sobbed. The new campus pastor, who I'd rapidly become best friends with over the past two years, was sitting on the sofa watching me. She finally, almost in a whisper, said, "You need to breathe, Rebecca. You need to breathe."

There's nothing easy about divorce. Even if you're not going through the trauma of realizing you have been married to a sociopathic narcissist who'd been manipulating and emotionally abusing you for years, divorce still is a painful thing. It's like the ripping apart of your soul, and for a while, you just hemorrhage and wonder if the bleeding will ever stop, or if you'll finally just be emptied of everything until it kills you.

Not to mention the anxiety. The nerve-shattering anxiety that soon would cause me to become overwhelmed in a grocery store because there were too many people and too many decisions to make and having to leave abruptly because I was having a panic attack. After that I shook for two days straight. I jumped out of my skin when the mailman came to the door. Apparently two years of receiving court documents in the mail made me dread the sound of the mailbox clank.

And the guilt. The utter, terrible guilt that just shatters you.

Once I gave the go-ahead to file the divorce paperwork, I knew he would get served in prison and would be told that he had no home to go to and would be arrested if he stepped foot on my property. To be fair, I wasn't expecting that part—that the divorce filing came with an automatic restraining order—and I spent the rest of the afternoon bawling as the reality of the finality of my actions sunk in.

Whenever he called, he worked his manipulative games. "I can work on changing, but only if you help me," laying any chance he had of getting help on me staying with him. I knew this tactic, and refused to fall for it.

Didn't make it easy, though.

I truly believe he saw the divorce coming, but my guilt was compounded by the fact that the week leading up to his getting served the paperwork, he had been put on suicide watch at the county jail. This meant he was in isolation and could not make phone calls out. From my end, the silence was a respite. Still, I had a rudimentary understanding of what those suicide watch conditions were like in jail. It had to be awful.

In the meantime, I had a conference to attend in Minneapolis. Life for me had not stopped. So while I was awaiting the paperwork to arrive at the jail, and for him to be released from isolation, a colleague of mine in a nearby town and I drove up together. I didn't talk much during the nine-hour drive to the Twin Cities, but was looking forward to seeing a lot of my seminary friends and having a little respite from the troubles in my life, only to have her car stall. In the rain. In the middle of the freeway. During five-o'clock rush-hour traffic. In the middle lane. With the odometer's last three digits stuck on 666.

Eventually a cop came and directed traffic and helped us push the car to the side as we waited for the tow truck.

The tow truck arrived—and then the tow truck proceeded to break down and dropped its transmission. So we had to wait for yet another tow truck.

I couldn't help but wonder if this wasn't a portent of things to come.

The next day as I was having lunch with a friend, my phone began to ring. From the Department of Corrections.

With shaking fingers, I slid the red "ignore" button across the face of my phone and didn't answer. For the next few hours, my phone rang every fifteen minutes.

Then, suddenly, the calls stopped.

I knew why. He'd received the divorce paperwork that also contained a restraining order so he could not contact me directly.

Like clockwork, the next call I got was from his parents.

That I also ignored.

Then an email from them, with a list of his demands.

Then one of his remaining friends called me.

Within just hours he'd begun the tactic of using others to come after me.

Upon returning home, I discovered from his brother that he had called his mother and began ranting and raving about how he was going to utterly destroy me professionally and financially.

This was not a complete shock. I'd been reading up on NPD's and had begun to half expect some of these tactics. The lengths that he would eventually go to, however, no one could have ever predicted. I eventually developed a saying: "Narcissists are predictable in their unpredictability. You know something crazy is coming, you just don't know what form of crazy it's going to take."

Still, despite all of this, I couldn't help feeling like I was abandoning him in his darkest hour. When I voiced this concern to my bestie over chips and queso—or as we had started calling it, liquid cheese—her response was simply: "Some of us don't know why you didn't divorce him the *first* time he went to jail."

Fair point.

It would take time for me to realize he abandoned me first and had subsequently forced his darkest hour onto me through his actions and decisions. While my head believed it, my heart had more trouble accepting that reality. Leaving him homeless, carless, and without a support system when he got out of prison just railed against my compassionate nature. Still, that aspect of my personality is also what he preyed upon and used to manipulate me and is what had kept me to this destructive cycle to begin with.

My grief, however, would eventually give way to fear and anger.

He would manage to shatter whatever remaining compassion and love I felt for him.

Eight
Puppet Master

> *"The puppet masters' only concern is how well they can manipulate their marionettes."*
>
> — Steven Redhead, *Life Is a Dance*

Probably the darkest fairy tale I've ever read was called "The Robber Bridegroom" by the Brothers Grimm. Short version: the bride discovers that her husband-to-be drugs, murders, and then eats women. She must use the severed finger of one of his victims to convince the guests at her own wedding that she shouldn't have to marry him.

Clearly a horrifying tale that one would not read to their children before bedtime.

I think about the realities of women during the time of the Brothers' Grimm, when girls were married off by their fathers and had no say in whom they married necessarily. I can only imagine what life might have been like to have been trapped in a marriage to a narcissist, sociopath or even a murderous psychopath like in the aforementioned fairy tale, with no way out. No resources, no careers, no escape.

It's surprising to me that more fairy tales don't prepare you for what happens when Prince Charming is a narcissist or sociopath. They prepare you for the evil stepmother, but not Prince Charming being the sociopath.

Not even Bible stories prepare you for this reality. I can go back now and maybe see some of the traits in some of the Biblical characters, but more often than not, we still view these people in a positive light. They're redeemable. We chalk it up to the culture that they lived in.

Therefore, there is nothing in your life if you didn't grow up in a family with narcissists in it that prepares you for what it's like to divorce a narcissist. Nothing. Until you go through it yourself, you still have no comprehension for just how completely unhinged, bizarre, and downright dangerous and weird it gets.

In the early days of my divorce proceedings while my soon-to-be-ex was still sitting in Leavenworth Prison, I took a trip to Key West with a friend to just get away from everything that was going on and discovered the Wyland Art Gallery that was dedicated to the contemporary artwork of Russian artist Michael Cheval. His art style was called "absurdist," though the topic is typically anything but. He uses characters usually dressed up in a medieval, Renaissance-style court with the puffy shoulders, large white ruff collars, placed in strange situations, like walking down a piano keyboard in the middle of an ocean. I felt an immediate pull to his styles and themes. I'm sure my attraction to this style had nothing at all to do with the utterly absurd reality I had been living in the past several months since filing for divorce. The amount of just crazy and insane things that would get thrown my way were too awful to even remember clearly.

According to Cheval's definition, absurdism is an inverted side of reality, a reverse side of logic that does not emerge from the dreams of surrealists or the realm of the subconsciousness. Rather, it is a game of imagination, where all ties are carefully chosen to construct a literary plot. Cheval says: "Absurdity, like any other genre, has its own rules. But it implies everything that is outlying of common rules and boundaries...Absurdism is an attempt to understand our life the way it truly is."

Life the way it truly is. Breaking boundaries, defying norms, inverted logic, its own rules, games of imagination tied together to form a fantastic story.

Identical with the absurd traits of an individual with a narcissistic personality disorder. Which is why I felt drawn to this genre of painting and began incorporating it into my own work.

A narcissist is the greatest of manipulators, much like a puppet master who pulls the strings of unsuspecting victims to dance at their whim. They enjoy playing with someone's mind as though it were just some big practical joke, as they gaslight you constantly.

Author Cherilyn Christen Clough once described gaslighting as like "having all of your memories touched up in photoshop—they alter them for you to the point you can't trust what you've been seeing and experiencing."[1] They then declare you're either crazy—or lying. Since you know you're not lying, the only option they leave available to you is that you must be crazy. Reality itself begins to unravel. They enjoy the game of playing with and manipulating simple facts and twist them into a pretzel to tie their victim's brain in knots. You begin to question your sanity if items keep moving around with no one else to validate your experience. Which is why they tend to isolate their puppets as much as possible. It becomes a game to see how far they can go in convincing their "puppet" that things are not as they seem.

For example, my husband once tried to convince me he had been diagnosed with cancer. I knew that was ridiculous, but he became so insistent, I started to believe it might be true. When I brought this alleged history of cancer up

---

1. Clough, Cherilyn Christen, "The Narcissist as Puppet Master: How to Survive Gaslighting Without Losing Your Mind," cherilynchristenclough.medium.com, 2019.

during a life insurance exam, he stared at me blankly and said he had no idea what I was talking about.

Gaslighting catches people off guard because it plays off their vulnerability. No one imagines they are in a loving relationship when they are being openly abused and bullied, but gaslighting can be so subtle that many victims don't recognize it as abuse until they're on the verge of losing their minds. What's so chilling and disturbing about gaslighting is that the puppet master often engages their puppet in a game without them even realizing it.

They don't realize it because narcissists wear a human mask. They have to in order to draw people into their game. I was "love bombed" when I first met my husband. Love bombing is when your partner bombards you with attention and barrages you with intense love and affection. All those movies I liked he suddenly wanted to watch because I liked them. Trips to vineyards, because it's something I liked. Even the mixed CD was to show how much he had been paying attention to the things I told him.

A narcissistic person love bombs so that the other partner can develop emotional, physical, or financial dependence on them. This is a learned pattern of behavior, where the narcissist's self-worth is so low that they overcompensate with love bombing so they can receive the reciprocated love and affection they need to maintain their self-worth. This is all part of their cycle of idealization and devaluation that is at the core of narcissistic behavior.

Those masks of humanity, those masks of empathy and love, eventually begin to crack and reveal the true self underneath: a stark white blank face with dark, soulless eyes. There is no empathy, no feeling, and nothing genuine or real. He is larger than life—an inflated sense of self that diminishes everyone around him.

I never really saw my husband as being someone who had an overinflated sense of ego, until I started looking at some of the subtle behaviors. He wasn't the type that would walk into a room and demand all the attention. Rather, he believed things like his work would not function without him. He was the absolute best at what he did, and no one was going to ever be better than him at it. Everyone else was stupid, and they were fools.

At the time, this just seemed like a bit of over-the-top confidence.

He loved WWE wrestling, which in and of itself was not unusual, but when he was among friends, he would walk into a room and make the exaggerated "Wooo!" like Ric Flair. We all would just roll our eyes, but I soon realized it's how he saw himself.

Of course, he was always smarter than the legal system he was battling. They were all stupid. They were all wrong. He was right; he just didn't have the money to fight the total injustice that was being done to him. It's not a coincidence that like Ted Bundy, he more than once attempted to represent himself in both federal court and divorce court. He went through multiple attorneys in both cases because they never represented him correctly or would do what he wanted them to do because he knew the law better than they did, clearly.

I soon realized he used his superficially charming personality to exploit the naïve and compassionate like myself. He delighted in questioning why he would have to do certain things that didn't align with his own personal sense of justice or right and wrong, but for the most part he tried to adhere to social norms. Though to be fair, he frequently only adhered to those social rules that he found acceptable. For example, screaming and yelling at people when he was angry with them, or they didn't do what he wanted, he didn't find problematic. Throwing items at someone because he was angry was a reasonable action. Social norms would say that behavior was scary and unpredictable. He saw it as totally normal, and therefore, there were no problems doing it. When others became appalled, irritated, or alienated by his behavior, he responded with surprise that others were appalled, and then rationalized and justified his actions.

He projected blame onto others—it was always his daughter, the judge, or the attorney's fault—and he would become resentful of any comments or actions that could be construed as personally derogatory. If I ever tried to point out where he might have been in error, he'd employ a self-righteous anger to fend off my detractions. It would be some time before I realized the underlying anxiety he felt at being exposed and shamed, and such rebuffs to his self-esteem disrupted his usual composure and elicited a range of unpredictable behavior such as anger, depression, or withdrawal.

My husband was never able to recognize what he'd ever done wrong, and was reluctant to identify faults within himself that others might readily admit to. He frequently would boast that he was Superman: nothing could kill him, and he never got sick. I used to think he was joking, but soon realized, he actually believed that about himself. He had a skewed view of reality, an inverted sense of right and wrong. From the threats he had made to walking away from the RRC facility, everything was always either warranted behavior, or they were the ones being unreasonable.

After all, it was not "reasonable" in his world that he should have to show up to a facility on Saturday and wait for the orientation on Wednesday before he would be allowed to leave. That was their failure—not his for not bothering to find out when the orientation was and arrange to arrive on a Wednesday instead of a Saturday. There was no acknowledgement that he'd been playing the system for as long as he could to avoid going in the first place. Because he believed he didn't belong there, that he'd done nothing to warrant the punishment he was now receiving. He was a victim of the legal system that had a vendetta out to get him.

All around him was a fantasy-like façade of grandness and splendor—but eventually, as with all narcissists, it began to crumble around him as the storm clouds gathered and the waves from the chaotic sea that surrounded his "kingdom" began to destroy the poorly built pillars and walls. Yet he was oblivious to the destruction around him, drinking his wine and continuing his games.

I tried to explain to him what all of his exploits were doing to me one time. During his four months of flying to Atlanta and Dallas in order to delay having to report to the RRC facility, I met up with him in Dallas one weekend and tried to explain that all of these games he was playing with the legal system trying to avoid his punishment were wreaking havoc with me emotionally. I had developed severe anxiety waiting for the next court order. I'd fallen into a deep depression. I begged him to simply go do what he needed to do to end all of this.

At first, he stared off in the distance, completely unfocused as though he hadn't even heard me. Then he eventually came back with he couldn't just do what they wanted. He was at the judge's whim. The judge could keep him in that facility indefinitely. I pointed out no he couldn't; it was a misdemeanor charge. He could only keep him there for up to one year, and if he behaved himself, he could get out sooner than that. The court order specifically stated that he would be re-evaluated in a few months.

No. He was adamant; the judge would keep him there indefinitely because he'd find a way to break the rules. They were all breaking the rules in order to punish him.

He was always the victim. Never the rule-breaker facing the consequences of his actions.

I asked at one point if he even cared what this was doing to me.

He again just stared out in the distance and took a sip of his wine and never answered.

The one time we met with a marriage counselor, she asked him whether or not he cared about how his actions reflected on me given I was a public figure in the community. His deadpan response was simply, "They're Christian. They have to understand and forgive."

Being drawn to Cheval's "absurdism," I began incorporating that style into my own artwork as I tried to capture this "absurd" reality of what I was going through. My *"Puppet Master"* painting was the first attempt I made at this, depicting my husband as the Joker stuck in his ridiculous top hat as a reminder that nothing about this person was real. The two of hearts floated between him and his puppet bride, a symbol of his duplicitous nature.

While he was busy playing his games, the bride took advantage of his momentary loss in concentration as she reached for scissors that had been carelessly lying about so she could cut her strings. Even though he was distracted, and he left her the means with which to break free, cutting the strings was no easy task as the scissors were large and would take everything she had to control them. And her window of opportunity was short.

For in the background, we could see that the ship had already set sail but was not so far away that rescue was not still possible before the waves overwhelmed the entire scene. Thus, there were only two escape paths — the roiling sea, or the stairs that spiral out of the scene on the other side. The stairs would in theory be the easier route—though it would take her in front of the puppet master so his sights might once again be set upon her as he would undoubtedly try and block her escape and re-attach the strings.

The other involved facing the chaotic storm and swimming to the rescue boat without drowning beneath the waves. Neither option was safe, but were the only ways through to freedom. For the world of the narcissist is falling apart and the bride can either remain tied to him and be crushed by the collapsing world he has constructed or take her chances trying to escape.

I was spending my time trying to figure out what the safest route was to get out of this marriage, knowing the four months that he'd been sentenced to in Leavenworth would be over soon and my window of opportunity was rapidly disappearing.

During my marriage, I was not able to fully see the manipulation that was going on. It wasn't until I was finally able to break free that I more clearly saw I'd been little more than a pawn in a larger game being played. He was the puppet master, and the rest of us were all puppets or game pieces for him to play with.

The realization soon began to dawn on me that my entire marriage had been nothing more than a means to an end. I provided security and a certain amount of protection while he was busy playing games with other people's lives. Even sitting in prison, he figured when he got out, I'd be there waiting for him. I was a pastor, after all, and wasn't supposed to divorce him. This had been what he felt would be his ace in the hole. I was a shield that kept the courts at bay to some degree.

In fact, they did not send him to Leavenworth until after I filed the divorce paperwork. They were trying to show some deference and compassion toward me, keeping him where I could visit him.

He knew this. He needed me.

Many of my friends, not just my bestie that day sitting across from me with liquid cheese, wondered why I stayed married as long as I did after the first round of arrests. Why did I stay another two years? The answer was pretty simple: I took vows. I took those vows seriously.

I knew I could not keep living the way I'd been living the past three years, but divorce? How could I do that either? I had to stand up in front of hundreds of people *every* weekend and talk about faith, commitment—all those things that were supposed to be a part of my marriage.

Yet, I found myself having to pen a letter explaining to the four hundred households in my congregation how my marriage had utterly failed.

Guilt. Shame. Embarrassment. That doesn't even touch the surface of emotions I was feeling.

Worse, he knew that I would feel those things. He knew he could manipulate those feelings were I to give him any chance to do so.

It took some time for me to realize that those vows I had taken had more than just one part to them. The part we tend to focus on when divorce enters the conversation is "for better or for worse until death parts us" and we think *"that was my vow. This is just the 'worse' part that we promised to see them through."*

Perhaps. But we seem to always forget that there was a first part to that vow. There was a promise to "love, honor and cherish, for better or for worse until death parts us."

This was not like life just got more difficult due to a health issue beyond anyone's control. This was a deep betrayal of the marriage vows from the get-go.

In many marriages, the first part of that vow, "to love, honor and cherish," is so egregiously violated, the second part becomes a moot point. Because if you're not loving, honoring, and cherishing the person you married, what did you promise to do?

I know I did not stand up there in front of my pastor and colleague on my wedding day and state, "I promise to put up with all sorts of lies, abuse, and manipulation until I'm a completely broken shell of a person, for better or for worse, until death parts us—because he literally killed me." Pretty sure that was *not* the vow I took.

Pretty sure the vow he took as well was a promise to love, honor and cherish me, too—and given that vow was broken the moment he said it because there was this pile of lies he was hiding from me, it made the rest of the vow null and void.

Now from his perspective, my filing for divorce was a complete and utter betrayal of those vows. He wrote letters to my senior pastor, council president, and bishop declaring that I had lied the day I took those vows. The mere act of filing for divorce meant I'd lied when I said for better or for worse. Yet another way in which one twists reality. The divorce was my fault, not his. I was the one doing all of the betraying by walking away.

Not that he'd been the one to betray every single part of our marriage with lies and deception from day one.

Marriage is by no means easy. Relationships are hard. Intimate relationships require a lot of trust, communication, and compromise. I'm not one who advocates for divorce simply because one is disappointed that the fairy tale didn't emerge exactly as expected, or that there are sometimes rough waters you need to travail.

Marriage, however, was always meant to be life-giving for both involved. A partnership where one edifies the other.

Marriage is not meant to be destructive toward either of the individuals involved. It may be difficult; it may get hard to see each other lovingly through difficult times.

It should not, however, be destructive and abusive.

People make mistakes in relationships. It's inevitable. Marriage does not mean there won't be mistakes, there won't be errors, there won't be things that you do that harm your spouse. That's going to happen. That's where forgiveness and love—by both parties—has to come in.

When the Bible describes the marital bond, it talks about serving one another out of reverence for Christ (Ephesians 5:21). It also states that men are to love their wives the same way they love themselves. They should not abuse themselves and likewise should not abuse their spouse.

Abuse comes in many forms. Physical. Emotional. Mental.

Thus there has to come a point where forgiving over and over for the same harmful thing, being beaten down, being made to feel on a regular basis like your life is spinning out of control for no better reason than your spouse can't seem to learn to follow *any* rules and cares about no one but himself, is leading you down a path that has destroyed you rather than edified you—that's when you need to realize your marriage is destructive and nothing good will come from you staying together. You are simply fulfilling his need for you to be a toy he can yank around at his whim. That you're just a chess piece in his weird and twisted game. You become less of a person at that point. You are not a partner; you are a pawn.

God did not create you—or marriage—so that you would spend your life as a game piece, as an anxious mess, fearful of the person you share your life and bed with, wondering when the narcissistic rage is going to become more than just word vomit and turn physically violent.

That's not a marriage. That's not a partnership. That's its own prison sentence into destruction.

And that is not the vow you took. The vow you both took was broken long ago. Dissolving the legality of that marriage at this point was just paperwork because it ceased being a marriage—or in some cases never really was a marriage—due to the deceptive nature of one of the participants. The vow was a lie from the start, and thus invalid.

I'm also pretty sure God's intention for marriage is that two whole people are brought together into a whole relationship. Sort of like multiplication. My therapist, the one who correctly pegged my husband as a sociopath, once explained it to me like this: $1 \times 1 = 1$. Two whole people equal a whole and healthy relationship. But when you only bring half of one person into a relationship: $1 \times 1/2 = 1/2$. God's intent is not that our relationship be only half a relationship, or if two halves are brought together, they only equal a quarter of a relationship. Or worse yet, when you try to combine a whole, healthy person with someone who is so deceptive that their entire being is a lie, then you get: $1 \times 0 = 0$. The whole person becomes broken down and negated by the vacuum and chaos of the other. Who they were as a person gets totally annihilated in the midst of this destructive relationship.

There literally is no relationship at that point. At least nothing that is recognizable in the way in which God intends human marital relationships. The relationship is dead.

"Until death parts us." Most of us think this death is physical death, but the death of the relationship is a real thing, too. It lies shattered on the pile of hurt and deception that's been building up.

Our entire relationship had been based on lies. Lies about the kind of person he was. Lies about why he had married me. Lies about even loving me.

I worked through these realities in my artwork. My marriage was absurd. It was an inverted reality. I was a puppet in the midst of a larger game being played by the "puppet master," chess and poker respectively. One was a game of strategy, the other a game of chance; always with some ace up his sleeve to show the propensity to cheat and try to control the outcome.

I was incredibly lucky compared to a lot of women trying to escape their puppet master narcissist. While my own escape was by no means easy—I did at least have some of the tools at my disposal to get away. There was a ship for me to board. A way out.

I had my own home that was not in his name from before we were married.

I had a career and a means of income that would sustain me.

I had friends and family that surrounded and supported me. If I needed financial help, I knew my parents would have helped me.

I lived in a smaller community where the local police kept an eye out for me.

I had people who believed me and didn't think I was the crazy one.

I had no children to tie me to him for the rest of our lives.

He was safely locked away in Leavenworth Federal Prison for four months so I could remove his stuff from my house and put it in a storage unit.

In the grand scheme of things, my "escape" was far "easier" than a lot of women's, who don't have jobs, have children to consider, and don't have the same support system in place. I honestly cannot imagine how they are even able to leave without those factors.

Because the moment I filed for divorce, whatever illusions I had about who he was came crashing down around me. Whatever love he once professed disappeared.

The day he received the divorce papers, rather than being sad and depressed, he called up his mother and angrily yelled, "I'm going to utterly destroy her!"

I had thankfully already taken the necessary steps of getting my name off his credit cards, closing out our joint bank accounts, and shifting my paychecks into a separate bank account.

Financially, he wasn't able to touch me.

So he set about trying to destroy me in the eyes of our community by having his friends post terrible things on Facebook about me with the hopes that my congregation members would see it and turn on me.

I remember sitting in Red Lobster one day with my best friend, the campus pastor, and seeing a post of his and was first of all floored by how that even happened: he was in prison. He must have gotten one of his friends to do it. The post went on to say how terrible it was that I, a pastor, was divorcing him. After all, he was not "in prison," he was only "in jail," as it was right before they shipped him off to Leavenworth. In his twisted mind, this was supposed to show me in a bad light, for divorcing him while he was at his lowest moment. That I wasn't being very "Christian" for a pastor.

The sad reality is that is exactly what I felt like I had done. He knew that. He knew he could manipulate that and exploit those feelings.

Just like when he tried to tell me that he needed me in order to get better. The only time he finally admitted he had a problem was when he realized I was on the verge of divorcing him. He called me from prison and said he knew he had a problem, but the only way he could get better is if I stayed with him and helped him with this therapy.

Just more manipulation.

I was so shocked by the post that I stood up and walked out of the restaurant without paying. Luckily my friend took care of the check by the time I finally regained my senses and walked back into the restaurant to pay the bill.

If I ever had any doubts that his marriage to me was nothing more than a farce and a giant manipulative game, those actions solidified it. I had simply been a puppet and a pawn in his bigger game of trying to avoid all of his legal ramifications.

Thus I soon realized, in my search for Prince Charming, I'd found the Robber Bridegroom instead.

Nine
Masquerade

"We all wear masks, and the time comes when we cannot remove them without removing some of our own skin."

— André Berthiaume

In the 1994 Disney movie *The Mask,* Stanley Ipkiss, played by Jim Carey, is a quiet, timid bank clerk who hates confrontation. One day, he discovers a mask which depicts Loki, the Norse god of mischief. When he puts it on, he becomes his inner self: a cartoon wild man. With the mask in place, he is able to be someone else and live out his more destructive inner desires.

The reality is, we all wear masks. Masks are used to either hide or establish an identity. To hide and reveal moods, thoughts, and personalities. We use them to both exaggerate and diminish.

Sometimes we want to hide who we really are behind a façade we want the world to see. Other times, we use the mask to hide deep pain and sorrow. Our masks are usually a better version of ourselves than we want to admit or face. Sometimes it's to put on a brave front—other times, to attract attention. We use them to deflect criticism, to not appear too proud or to show how much something has hurt. Some masks are far more elaborate than others—but there nonetheless. We use them to hide not only from others, but many times from ourselves. For when the mask is in place, even looking in a mirror reflects what we want it to.

We use masks to highlight the things we want seen, to magnify the parts of ourselves we are proud of or who we would like to be.

We use them to fit in. To make others think we're like them. Sometimes we are. Sometimes—not so much.

They're also our defense. Our safety. Masks ward off danger, keeping the world at bay. Because seeing the true identity of who the real person is that lies beneath is scary. Our flaws, our mistakes, our pain, our sorrow, our regrets, our insecurities—when unmasked, these things make us vulnerable. When admitted to others, we risk judgment, we risk others changing their opinions of who they think we are. At times we risk friendships and relationships when the mask is lowered. No matter how "real" we think we are—there is always something we're hiding. There is always something about ourselves we don't want others to know. Guilt. Shame. Fear. Sin. Pain. Ego. Pride. Addictions. Abuse. Sorrow. Silent hells.

As a pastor, I see a lot of masks—and at times I am privileged enough to see when the mask is lowered and catch a glimpse of the person underneath, if even for a short time.

I wear my own masks. I know they're there. I cling to them for protection. I wear them because sometimes, what lies beneath is too broken to unveil. Just like I see many masks on others being a pastor, I must wear many masks in that same role. Keeping silent when I want to scream. Staying calm when everything in my being wants to run for the hills. Smiling when I want to cry. Staying serious when I want to laugh hysterically.

Life is a juggling act most of the time. Especially as you grow older. For women in particular, there is a sense of time running out as certain dreams for your life begin to wind down as our bodies change and certain realities hit home. Career, relationships, family, and the ticking biological clock can all figure in. For many we reach a stage in our life where we feel our dreams are slipping away with the passage of time and age. A sense of urgency overwhelms us and sometimes results in a narrative we tell ourselves. A narrative that results in decisions we later regret.

Yet we wear a mask of wisdom (the peacock feather is a symbol of insight and wisdom) as we try to juggle the desires of our heart against the ticking clock. We "wisely" tell ourselves that nothing in life is perfect, so compromise is okay.

Surely that is wisdom.

For so much of our life, we've made prudent decisions, shown a depth of insight into so much of what we say and do. This is how others see us, and how we begin to see ourselves.

Yet it is only a mask. A display of beauty and grace, as though everything is just as it should be.

Perfect.

Methodical.

Unmoving.

The underlying reality, however, is that emotions affect our biology and health and are not just a "state of feeling." They actually alter how the brain functions. In particular, living in states of stress or anxiety for prolonged periods of time changes brain activity and connections. This alters how we think, our memories, and even behavior.

Whatever "wisdom" we appear to exude when it comes to matters that involve our hearts and deepest yearnings, when it comes to the things in life that can matter the most, it just masks the reality that at our core, we are hurting, broken people that at times can allow ourselves to be used, manipulated and abused. "You're too smart for that" are words that haunt us, wondering how we didn't have the insight and wisdom to see what we knew was there.

So we wear a mask, trying to hide our mistakes, hide the emotion that clouds the wisdom we so desire, hoping it won't be ripped off again to reveal the vulnerability that lies beneath. That we won't again let the mask fall away. That the lie we tell ourselves about ourselves won't be revealed for what it is.

For some of us, it's called "imposter syndrome." We fear that at our core, we are not what we present ourselves to be. That someone will find out we're not as smart, gifted or talented as everyone seems to think we are. Our insecurities lie behind this mask, believing we aren't as good or as qualified as the world lauds us. Women, in particular, suffer from this imposter syndrome, worried that even though they are likely far more qualified than their male peers, they will be held to a much higher standard of perfection and worry that they won't live up to a standard that is not even remotely expected of their male colleagues.

One way or another—our lives are intimately affected by the masks we wear.

Our masks are only removed fully and completely when we stand before God—who sees into our hearts and past what we want to show the world, and ourselves. In the end, no matter how many masks we wear, the only identity that ultimately matters is the one assigned to us by Christ—"child of God."

While many of the masks we wear we use to protect ourselves, masks at times can be harmful, too.

Yes, we all have them to hide some of the bad things we don't want others to see, some wear a mask of "sanity" to hide the "insanity" that lies within. They are outwardly a perfect mimic of a normally functioning person, able to mask or disguise the fundamental lack of internal personality structure and their internal chaos that results in repeatedly purposeful destructive behavior.

All sociopaths/narcissists wear a mask. I'm going to use the terms sociopath and narcissist rather interchangeably here, mainly because while there are nuanced differences, they both present in much the same way. Their behaviors tend to be very similar, just their overall motivation may differ. A sociopath tends to actually enjoy hurting others, whereas a narcissist is merely indifferent to the hurt and pain they cause so long as it helps them achieve their goal. Sociopaths struggle to understand or connect with others' emotions, often viewing them as tools to be manipulated for personal gain. Narcissists may display more variability in their capacity for empathy. While they generally lack empathy, they can exhibit moments of empathy, especially when it serves their self-interest or enhances their self-image.

Sociopaths engage in impulsive and reckless behavior, often disregarding consequences and exhibiting a pattern of irresponsibility. They may also show a history of criminal activity or a disregard for social norms.

Narcissists tend to be more calculated in their actions and maintain a carefully crafted image. They may engage in manipulative tactics to achieve personal goals or maintain their inflated self-image.

Sociopaths land in the "anti-social" personality disorder section on the Axis II DSM (Diagnostic and Statistical Manual of Mental Disorders) scale, while narcissists have their own designation of narcissistic personality disorder. As my therapist said: it's a sliding scale.

It is difficult to say whether my ex-husband was a narcissist or a sociopath as he displayed traits from both disorders. While he was not diagnosed with anti-social traits, part of that is because I know, after reading the answers he gave when interviewed for his psychological evaluation, he lied about certain urges, impulses, and desires as he knew they would be red flags.

Ultimately what this means is the person that you see and experience is not the person they actually are. They are able to be different things with different people. They have a stunning ability to quickly assess somebody and be everything that they want and need. To do this, they use charismatic charm.

A narcissist/sociopath will always assess you. You will watch them staring at you. When unnerved at why they are staring at you, they will say something like 'I am just looking at how beautiful you are.' They say it with such sincerity, you can hardly believe that someone would use such a cheesy line and think they can get away with it. But a narcissist/sociopath does. They will charm the birds out of the trees because they are masters of charm.

That mask will always remain in place until they fly into a fit of narcissistic rage. Once the rage is over, the mask slides back into place as though nothing had happened. All narcissists will eventually let the rage loose, and the mask will slip. But then they'll turn around and gaslight you into thinking whatever you just saw—you didn't really see.

I still remember the first time I witnessed that rage and the mask slipping—only to watch it slide right back into place as though nothing had ever happened.

I walked into the house and could hear him screaming and yelling at someone on the phone. I don't even remember over what anymore. A credit card company probably. I froze in the doorway, not comprehending what I was seeing and hearing. I mean, I'd heard people yell before, but this, this was something else entirely. It's hard to describe the intensity, vulgarity, and rapid-fire way in which they yell and berate. It's designed to not allow the other person to argue or fight back, to keep them off balance as they switch from one topic of rage to the next.

Then he slammed the phone down and turned toward me, smiling and completely calm as though two seconds earlier he hadn't been red-faced and screaming like a mad man at the customer service agent on the other end of the line. He leaned over and kissed me, smiling as he asked, "So, how was your day, honey?"

I blinked in astonishment. What had I just witnessed?

When I'm angry enough to yell at someone, I can't just suddenly turn that anger on and off. I'd be simmering and stewing and would immediately be telling my significant other exactly what had happened and why I was in such a tizzy. It takes a while for me to cool down after an encounter such as that.

There is none of that with a narcissist. Just the mask sliding back into place as though nothing out of the ordinary or strange had just occurred. I remember physically shivering as a chill ran down my spine at how quickly he could pivot his emotions.

Then there was the issue with the cable company. We'd been having trouble with our modem and internet speed. He'd called and requested a technician come out and deal with the problem. The technician came out and began trying to explain that we needed to use their modem instead of the modem my husband had bought.

He lost it. Absolutely lost it. He began screaming and yelling at the technician, and at one point even threw the modem at him. I shrank back in horror. When it was finally all over and the technician left, I tried to confront him on his outlandish behavior.

Somehow, by the end of the evening, he'd convinced me that his reaction was perfectly normal and this was simply how you had to deal with people or they would always take advantage of you. This may be, but throwing modems at them seemed a bit harsh.

Or the time we were trying to return something at Walmart. He got angry when they wouldn't take it back without the proper receipt and literally threw the item at the clerk and stormed out of the store.

Or when he would fight with his daughter. The screaming and the yelling. The constant barrage of profanity and not allowing the other person to even get another word in edgewise.

Maybe the worst was with the insurance company after our basement flooded. They were refusing to paint the entire wall after six inches of water had filled the entire basement and ruined the dry wall. It was ridiculous that they would only cover painting the bottom half of the walls.

He got on the phone with them, and for the next half hour unleashed a barrage of screaming and yelling that wouldn't allow anyone to get a word in edgewise. When he was finished, he simply slammed the phone down and ended the conversation. The rest of us sat on the line in silence for a moment before the insurance agent finally went, "That was insane. You know that, right?"

Yes. I knew that. Yet, I had started growing accustomed to it, sadly.

The truly terrifying part was always that he would then turn to me and be completely and perfectly calm, as though nothing out of the ordinary had just happened. When I'd get upset, he'd tell me I was overreacting.

Oh the irony of being told *I* was the one overreacting.

It didn't help that my family and friends had never really seen this side of him, so when I would say that he tended to yell at people in customer service a lot, they agreed that sometimes people deserved to be yelled at. This didn't seem right to me, but everyone else seemed to think it was normal and fine, so I began to normalize it myself.

I soon found myself constantly walking on eggshells, not wanting to do anything to incur those tirades. I had begun at this point to truly question who and what I'd married, all the legal issues aside. It, of course, got worse after his arrest. Anything could set him into a tirade.

Without charm, you wouldn't be interested in a sociopath. They need charm and lies, and the mask that they wear, to gain your trust. They use their mask of charm to continue to control you, and abuse you. Without this, if you knew the actual truth about the sociopath, you would probably never be interested in him in the first place.

It can be difficult to come to terms with the fact that this is not who this person is at all. The mask is the mask of humanity and kindness. The mask will do kind things for people. They will seem caring, give money to friends in need, volunteer to help with whatever thing you might need done. They will particularly utilize the church to carry out their seemingly benevolent and kind behavior.

Still, it's only a mask, hiding the sociopath underneath. Someone who is selfish, uses people, has no care for the rights or welfare of others. Someone who is only doing all those nice things to later somehow use them against you. But of course, if you knew this, you would never have become involved with them in the first place. The mask is a necessity for them to lure people in.

The flip side is that masks are also many times necessary for survival and self-preservation. I had begun to wear my own mask—the mask I tried to show to everyone else that everything was fine.

I don't know if my masks were nearly as effective as his were, but I would show up to worship every weekend and smile and preach and behave like there was nothing at all wrong in my life. When I spoke to my friends, I tried hard not to let the stress of our home situation show.

My mask only worked to a certain degree. After I filed for divorce, I received a letter from a parishioner that stated, "we are so sorry to hear about your divorce, but we have all seen the changes in you. You have not been our lovely Rebecca for some time. We hope you will be able to return to us now."

That note, more than anything, caused me to break down. The past two years of hell I'd been living had been *that* obvious? My mask had apparently not been as effective as I'd hoped.

Well, to be fair, I'd become a shadow of myself, barely recognizing my own reflection. The stress had indeed taken a physical toll as much as an emotional one. I guess I just didn't realize that what I saw in the mirror, everyone else was seeing as well. They knew. They could see it.

My mask had failed.

Ten
Down the Rabbit Hole

"It's a great huge game of chess that's being played—all over the world—if this is the world at all, you know."

— Alice, *Through the Looking Glass*

LEWIS CARROLL WROTE HIS books *Alice in Wonderland* and *Through the Looking Glass*, to describe the "absurdity" of where he felt mathematics was going in his day with things like "imaginary numbers." As mentioned before, the absurd nature of a narcissist was why I was drawn to the absurdist style of Michael Cheval's art—a game of imagination, where all ties are carefully chosen to construct a literary plot, implying everything that is outlying of common rules and boundaries as an attempt to understand our life the way it truly is. Likewise, Carroll's Wonderland is a world that transforms with its own unique logic that thwarts Alice's expectations at every turn.

Throughout my marriage, and especially during the divorce process, I felt less like a princess who had found her Prince Charming, and more like Alice who fell down the rabbit hole and was walking through a messed-up Wonderland of chaos and absurdity.

When you live with an individual with a narcissistic personality disorder, you enter into a world that defies logic, that defies the rules and laws of "normal" human behavior. The more one delves into certain realms of the narcissist in their life, the more chaotic and unreal everything becomes. Life is turned upside down, everything you think you know is dumped on its head. There is typically a "rabbit hole" of paperwork that reveals a pathology and pattern of behavior so twisted that the more you discover, the deeper and deeper you fall into the confusion and surreal nature of what you have unwittingly gotten yourself involved in. You are caught in a game that you don't know the rules to and fall into a world that is foreign and strange.

I did not know, or understand, the full extent of the things my husband had done to land himself into the kind of trouble that eventually got him shipped off to Leavenworth Federal Prison. It was while he was safely locked away that I began the process of going through the boxes and boxes of paperwork that were stored in my basement that contained all the court documents, copies of emails and letters that were sent, and of course all of his financials.

I could not face the overwhelming task of going through them myself. Even if I could, I lacked the skills and financial background to even know what I was looking at. Instead, I had a friend who was a former anti-money-laundering specialist going through the financial aspect of it and piecing together the story of my soon-to-be-ex-husband's past.

It was a trail of documents, court cases, and financial records dating back to 1994. Financial records tell you a lot about a person, and this was no exception. His financials were a world of crazy madness that started long before his troubles with the mortgage he'd defaulted on. It also revealed a web of lies he'd spun, the narrative about his life he wanted others to believe that stood in stark contrast to reality.

Bankruptcy, multiple claims of identity theft with the IRS (there was no identity theft—those claims were what he repeatedly filed after he lost a fight with them), getting fired from his job at the Marriott because he had purchased a PlayStation with the company credit card then tried to claim he'd bought it with his mother's employee discount from Walmart—and that was just the beginning.

There were multiple domestic abuse complaints that had been filed from ex-girlfriends, and death threats made against a lot of people.

Narcissists are, by nature, masters of twisting logic around to fit their imaginary world. The lies and fantasy become so real to them, they actually believe it themselves. They reinvent reality to fit their personal agenda.

Dr. Sam Vaknin, in the *Journal of Addiction and Addictive Disorders* writes,

> "*Narcissists and psychopaths dissociate a lot because their contact with the world and with others is via a fictitious construct: The false self. Narcissists never experience reality directly but through a distorting lens darkly. They get rid of any information that challenges their grandiose self-perception and the narrative they had constructed to explicate, excuse and legitimize their antisocial, self-centered and exploitative behaviors, choices and idiosyncrasies. In an attempt to compensate for the yawning gaps in memory, narcissists and psychopaths confabulate: They invent plausible "plug ins" and scenarios of how things might, could, or should have plausibly occurred. To outsiders, these fictional stopgaps appear as lies. But the narcissist fervently believes in their reality: He may not actually remember what had happened—but surely it could not have happened any other way! These tenuous concocted fillers are subject to frequent revision as the narcissist's inner world and external circumstances evolve. This is why narcissists and psychopaths often contradict themselves.*"[1]

They sadly suck others into this reinvented reality and are able to convince their targets that the absurd is somehow normal. There is just enough truth mingled into the fantasy that they are able to persuade others that this bizarre realm they are describing might actually exist.

When you begin to believe this fantasy world yourself—you normalize their behavior.

The angriest I ever became was the day my therapist informed me I'd been brainwashed into normalizing some of his aberrant behavior. I'd begun defending some of his outlandish actions by justifying them—the same way

---

1. Vaknin, Sam, "Dissociation and Confabulation in Narcissistic Disorders," HSOA Journal of Addiction and Addictive Disorders, Vol. 7, Issue 2, 2020, p. 2.

he tended to justify them. It was normal to yell and scream at people when you were angry. Sometimes people just deserved to be yelled at. Customer service people were infuriating, and they were not doing their jobs properly. Where was the accountability?

It hadn't helped matters that when I'd expressed dismay at this behavior, even my mother had defended his actions, despite the fact that she'd never seen him "in action." Whatever she had apparently been imagining was not what I had witnessed. Still, perhaps I was too sensitive.

So I'd begun to normalize the screaming and the yelling. It's what other people apparently did, and I was just the weak, non-confrontational one who squirmed uncomfortably when people's voices were raised.

Still, to suggest I'd been brainwashed was infuriating. I was a smart woman. Surely I couldn't be brainwashed!

My anger didn't last long as I was able to eventually reflect on her point and realize that she was correct. I had been brainwashed.

Narcissists force you to talk about them, even when you're condemning what they did. They're like a black hole that sucks your time, energy, and attention away from everything else and distorts your reality.

I fell into this black hole, past the event horizon, and into a realm where I couldn't see what was real and what wasn't. I was well into the brainwashing by this juncture.

It was such an ugly term, though. It's what cult leaders did. Then I realized, I shared a lot in common with those who fell prey to cult leaders.

While the grooming process is similar, so is how they pick their targets.

Most members of a cult are drawn in because they have a deep need and desire to be loved and accepted.

I was ripe for the manipulation. Given my previous relationships, my dreams, my desires, I simply wanted to believe that someone could love me—someone could wholly and completely love me the way he seemed to. The way he paid attention to things I liked, the way he would go out of his way to make sure we were doing something I enjoyed. I wanted more than anything to believe this could be true.

Plus, when we met, my dreams of a husband and a family were rapidly evaporating. It had been a decade since I'd experienced any sort of true affection from a man. I'd earned a master's degree, owned two homes, and changed careers in that time frame.

I hate to admit that I was feeling desperate, but...I was feeling desperate. That biological clock was ticking. My window of opportunity to have the fairy tale, that family I had always dreamed of, was quickly slipping away.

So when he walked into my life, totally accepted what I did for a living, and in fact encouraged and liked that aspect of my life, I clung to those things. Faith, he claimed, was important to him, so my being a pastor was not an issue.

We wanted the same things—children, a family, a life with someone special. Little did I know he was simply mimicking and mirroring my desires as a way to lure me in.

Admittedly, I was willing to overlook certain behaviors that might have otherwise seemed like red flags. I'd gotten glimpses of the rage one night when he'd fought with his daughter about a week after we got engaged. Like with the credit card company incident, when he returned to me, he was all calm and sweet and acted like just a few moments earlier he hadn't been a raving madman.

It bothered me, and I did at this juncture begin to question whether marrying him was the right move.

It was over Memorial Day weekend, and I left angry and upset, telling him I really needed to think and reconsider things. But he wore me down. He drove the three hours back to Kearney to stand on my doorstep when I'd refused to take his calls because I needed time alone to think. He wouldn't let me have that time. He needed to defend himself, to manipulate me, to explain things.

Admittedly it was the being able to turn those emotions on a dime that should have been my warning signal, but there was a pattern to the kind of men I seemed to be attracted to, or that I seemed to attract, and thus I had long ago normalized these things. He was never overtly violent toward me, but he definitely had a violent and volatile streak. That violence had never landed on me, however, so I didn't see it as anything particularly dangerous in our relationship.

That's just how men behaved sometimes.

Men got angry. They got violent.

Many women become desensitized to this if they grew up in a violent household. That was not the case with me. My own father had not been a violent man at all. He rarely raised his voice, and when he did, you *knew* you were in deep trouble. To elicit a raised voice from my father meant you had crossed a very serious and terrible boundary.

In my eighteen years under their roof, I could count on one hand the number of times my father yelled at me. He could be cold and brusque at times, but never openly hostile or verbally abusive.

So angry, volatile, screaming men was not what I was accustomed to growing up. However, due to my dating experiences, I had just come to believe that my father was the exception, not the rule.

Given my husband was also very good at manipulating the evidence of what he had done that had landed him into legal trouble, I deduced I was simply making something out of nothing. Now, however, I was able to finally see the original court documents and discover what it was he had actually done.

It was not a misdemeanor; it was a felony that he had pled down to a misdemeanor. His "anger" at both the mortgage company he had been dealing with and the HUD (Housing and Urban Development) official were, it turned out, chilling threats.

He had threatened HUD with some of the following:

> *"Anyone comes to my home and attempts to enter will be hospitalized or worse...not a threat, a guarantee."*

> *"I will hospitalize anyone that trespasses on my property as a perceived threat."*

> "I will be in Oklahoma next week and can meet you at your office or at your home. Let me see you ignore me when I am standing at your front door or sitting with your wife and kids waiting for you to come home."

That last one had the individual's home address attached to it, and was therefore the one that got him in real trouble. As it should have. I remember feeling sick to my stomach as I read it, thinking of the horror of what it would feel like to have someone send you their home address so that you knew they knew where you lived, and then state that one day you would find them in your home with your family. That was really the piece that clarified how dangerous this man truly was.

As for the mortgage company, he'd offered up the following threats to their attorney:

> "If you try to get into my house, something will happen to the house of anyone who is involved."

> "Based on what they have done to me, if I were to die from this it would not be suicide, it would be manslaughter or murder. I'd push for first degree murder as [the mortgage company] is aware of what they are doing, as are you, and rather than stopping you are pushing harder and harder. That shows intent and premeditation. What if you pushing goes the other way? What if you push too far and someone snaps? Going on a rampage? Whose conscience is that on? Please note, this is not a threat or something I am concerned about me doing, but given the eleven-hundred complaints, plus comments on numerous articles, it is something I could see happening."

> "By Monday it will be too late, and things will be in motion that I will be unable to stop that will ultimately destroy [mortgage

company] and will do so legally. This isn't a threat of violence or harm—make no mistake. I will not be storming [the mortgage company's] headquarters."

That's also when I discovered some of the other protection orders and reports of domestic violence from a previous girlfriend that had made it to trial.

Three of my friends sat me down to go over that last bit, to try and drive home the kind of physical danger I had been in as well. The throwing knives I found in his nightstand took on a whole new meaning at this point. Along with the million-dollar life insurance policy he'd taken out on me. (Oh, my parents flipped out about that one when they found out.)

Reading those statements was like someone kicked me in the stomach. I went home and proceeded to throw up.

How often had I defended him? How often had I been outraged at how the courts were treating him? How often had I told the probation officer that they misunderstood him, that he wasn't at all dangerous? His bark was worse than his bite, I'd said on multiple occasions.

I could feel all of those lies I'd been told, and that I'd helped perpetuate, come tumbling down around me. That I had been thrown into his fantasy world and had begun to believe his fantasy was reality. Embarrassment didn't begin to describe what I was feeling.

Embarrassment. Betrayal. Heartache. Fear.

My friend, the anti-money laundering specialist, had begun the process of piecing together his financial history. Every week he would call me and say, "I know you feel guilty about filing for divorce while he's in jail. But I'm telling you—you're doing the right thing. He's still crazy."

When you begin the process of separating the fact from the fiction, and the more you realize and discover, the stranger it gets. Every time you think you have hit the bottom, something new rears its head and you find yourself falling once again. Every time you think there is an end to something, some new twist arises. This keeps everyone around them off-balance.

Narcissists are playing a game that they intend to win, no matter what the cost. Once the mask is ripped off, the truth of who they are is revealed, and all pretenses are dropped—the more vicious and dangerous the game becomes.

It is hard to convey in words what this feels like, but Lewis Carroll's descriptions of Alice trying to play games with the Queen of Hearts is as close as I can come. The rules shift. The game is maddening because it's not a fair game to begin with and produces anxiety and fear in the one trying to play against the Queen—who is constantly calling for everyone's decapitation.

Like the Queen, the narcissist, once revealed, comes off looking eventually like nothing more than the court jester to everyone around them as they make their demands and spin their tales. Yet they still have the power to evoke fear and exert a certain amount of control due to their unstable nature. Chaos is their greatest tool.

For the one who is targeted, this joker is a deadly serious character, and drags them into a "comedic hell."

Life is indeed absurd, but also very dangerous, in this world. Things spin out of control rapidly and as you fall, you cannot grasp walls or anything that seems stable to ground you and stop the free-fall into this crazy Wonderland. The past, the present, the future—time itself—become warped and twisted.

Like Alice's fall, there is eventually a bottom you hit that leads into this bizarre realm of reality that must be gone through in order to find your way back out again.

I had hit my bottom. Now I needed to find my way out.

Eleven

Saving Grace

"Sometimes being a friend means mastering the art of timing. There is a time for silence. A time to let go and allow people to hurl themselves into their own destiny. And a time to prepare to pick up the pieces when it's all over."

— Octavia Butler

Princess Aurora and Snow White were both put to sleep by evil witches. They woke up to find their handsome prince ready and waiting for them. They literally got to sleep through all the drama that unfolded around them and woke up to their happily ever after.

You don't know how many times I prayed for a fast forward button, or the ability to just go to sleep and wake up one day and have this all be in the past. Unfortunately, sleeping through the drama of life isn't how life works. You have to dig deep and find ways to keep going…or you die.

You have to get up each and every day, take a breath, and try to get through each minute, each hour.

I don't think I could have gone through with this whole divorce process without the support of my friends, family, colleagues, and congregation. Life during this time period made me feel as though I was drowning. I had given everything I had to give, was utterly exhausted emotionally and mentally, and felt the waves of life enveloping me as I sank further and further down into the depths of watery chaos. It was only the support and love of many friends and family that kept me from submerging into the dark abyss.

The campus pastor who had become one of my closest friends in town I have to give a special kind of shout out to. Not only was she a constant source of support, but her own life was affected by my situation in strange ways.

Due to the fact that our husbands shared the same first name, our Biblically-derived names both started with the same letter, and we were the only two female pastors in a town of thirty thousand people, I warned her people were likely to confuse the two of us. She brushed off the likelihood, until one day I got a call from her going, "You were right."

At least three people had chased her down in various parking lots thinking she was me, offering to pray for her situation. They were so earnest and well-meaning; she didn't have the heart to tell them she wasn't me.

These people really were my saving grace. The true hands and feet of Christ grabbing hold of me and not letting me go.

My faith sustained me during this time. I knew Christ was holding on to me with dear life. In my world, the hands of Christ came in many forms. Other people who were Christ to me, holding on to me and refusing to let go.

That is how this whole faith thing works for me. Christ works in and through the people around me, giving me the strength to get up each morning, take another breath, take another step. This is what community and relationship is about. It's what being the body of Christ for each other is about.

And it is what salvation is about. Christ reaching in and grabbing hold of me when I'm drowning. Who saves me and pulls me out of the depths of sin, despair, and chaos. All I can do is have faith he never lets go. Because he is my lifeline, my saving grace that keeps me from being overwhelmed by the tumultuous circumstances of life, even as I grope and gasp for the surface. I know I will never break free on my own. I know the tides of sin and our broken world will at times be too much to handle and fight against. I know I will succumb to the forces in this world that keep me from walking on top of the water, from weathering the storm. Instead, I sink and cry out "Save me!" Just like Peter in the story of Jesus walking on water, and Peter jumping out of the boat to greet him. As he, too, walked on water, he suddenly became aware of the storm that was lashing all around him and began sinking beneath waves, calling out "Save me!"

When I was in the sixth grade, I nearly drowned due to a strong undertow in Destin, Florida. One moment I was walking out into the ocean holding my mother's hand—the next I was ripped from her grasp and found myself being tossed wildly about by the waves in water where I could no longer touch the bottom.

I didn't realize what had happened exactly, it occurred so rapidly. All I knew was I could see the bottom, and I just kept swimming towards shore. But every time I put my feet down thinking I could stand, the undertow would grab me and pull me further out to sea. I eventually grew tired, battling against the crashing waves and watching as the shoreline grew more and more distant.

Now I was a pretty decent swimmer, even in the sixth grade. Thank goodness. It kept me from immediate demise. However, I didn't know at the time that the best thing to do was to just lift my legs and let the waves carry me in. So I unwittingly battled against forces I could not win against. They were invisible, but no less deadly.

I was rescued eventually by my father who floated out to me on a raft. He was not a great swimmer. But he knew something I didn't—I needed to be on top of the waves to survive. He grabbed hold of my tired and exhausted arm and told me not to worry; he would bring me in on the raft.

When I arrived back on shore, exhausted, I found my mother on the beach, sobbing. She thought I had drowned, overcome by the forces of the ocean neither one of us had any ability to control.

Life is the same way. There are forces around me that I do not always clearly see that threaten to drag me further and further out to sea; pulling me under and threatening to drown me before I'm even aware of what's happening. So often I think I have firm ground to stand on, but it's only an illusion and trick of refracting light and shadow. I'm further away from solid footing than I realize. And I am far more reliant on my perceived capabilities than I should be, when I am many times simply at the whim of nature and life with no control and no means to combat the invisible forces, until someone grabs hold and pulls me to shore. I exhaust myself as I fight and struggle.

I have to repeatedly tell myself: "Let go." Allow the hands of those around me to lift me up when I need them. Cry for help. And allow myself to be helped and saved. Get on top of the waves and just ride it out.

This is what my friends were to me. They saved me. They got me through the worst of this. They were my life raft.

My husband had thankfully been unable to isolate me from my friends like so many narcissists are apt to do. They were there to grab hold of my hands and refused to let me sink into the abyss.

This is not the case for so many women in my position. Many of them have been successfully isolated from their friends and family, or the narcissist in their life has succeeded in convincing everyone around her that she is the crazy one and out of line. They have nowhere to turn. Even their faith community may turn on them and blame them no matter what the circumstances. Or worse yet, tell them to return and forgive the abuse. Such situations truly break my heart, as that is not the point or the purpose of a faith community when you're dealing with divorce—especially divorce from someone who has abused you, cheated on you, or abandoned you.

I can't imagine I would have survived without that support system. It would have been worse than hell to try and navigate.

When I told one of my pastor friends I was filing for divorce, his immediate response was "Good." I couldn't help but let out a little laugh at that response. I knew, deep down, had I been a third-party observer, I'd have told myself to get out of this marriage two years earlier.

One of my bridesmaids, prior to my getting married, had taken me out to dinner to have a bit of a heart to heart and to express her concern about my marrying him. Everyone had already seen the challenges I was facing with the daughter. I was at a loss with how to deal with her, and when my friend asked me whether I was really sure about this wedding, I had to admit that the daughter concerned me. But, I reasoned, she was seventeen. She'd be out of the house soon. I could endure anything for a few years.

She additionally pointed to a court case she had seen about him. I waved it off. It was a simple misdemeanor from five years ago and was over and done with. Nothing to be concerned about. I was a pastor, after all. I was all about forgiveness and giving people second chances and not holding their pasts against them. It was hardly the first time I'd dated someone with a past. In fact, I'd yet to date someone who hadn't had some run-in with the law.

Besides, I was hardly super innocent. In the fourth grade, I discovered a cigar box in the closet in our spare room that was full of quarters and dimes in rolls. I truthfully thought I'd run across the equivalent of buried treasure. So I shared it with the neighbor girl and we both proceeded to buy, I kid you not, Weekly Reader books with the money. True crime material right there. Her parents thought it was strange she was paying for everything in quarters and dimes so they asked her where she got the money. She told them. Her parents called my parents, and the end result of that scenario was my parents took me down to the police station to try and "scare me straight." Honestly, it worked. Though I still felt a certain amount of injustice as I really hadn't realized I'd been stealing from anyone as I didn't know who the coins belonged to. Turned out they were part of a priceless coin collection my mother owned, so as an adult, I understand the gravity of the amount of money that was involved now. Still, I was probably twenty-one before I realized I didn't actually have a juvenile record, as my parents had recruited cop friends just to scare me, and I was never really brought up on charges.

So the red flags weren't flying on this for me, even if they should have been. We all make mistakes.

What I didn't do, and this is the advice I would like to give to every single woman who has friends who care enough to question their choice in a partner or spouse, was get angry with her. In fact, I thanked her for caring enough to express this concern. I was the opposite of angry. I even understood her concerns, and had it not been *my* heart that was involved, I'd have probably said the same thing. Note for the future: if it's something you'd say to someone else, then maybe you ought to listen.

When I got home, I texted her to reaffirm I was not angry, and I was very grateful to have a friend like her trying to look out for me.

In retrospect, I should have listened. My other word of advice to women? Listen to your friends. They know and they see things. Their hearts are not overriding their brains.

As I listened to the friend who responded with "good" as I told him about my filing for divorce, I admitted that a part of me knew that if I stayed with him, that might cost me my friendships. He said, "No, we wouldn't stop being your friend. But it would have meant you had consciously decided to choose crazy."

Telling my friends was one thing. Telling my congregation? That was another beast all together. Words do not describe the fear and trepidation I felt as I had to pen a letter to my congregation explaining why I was getting divorced. Yet, I had to get ahead of the curve. I couldn't let someone else control the narrative of what was going on in my life.

Not once did I mention the legal troubles in the letter I sent out. I simply stated that my marriage was broken beyond repair and to please respect our privacy during this heart-breaking time.

And then I sat back and waited for a few days. Would they demand I resign? Divorce is allowed in my denomination, but you never know how parishioners are going to respond when it's *their* pastor going through it. Did I need to find a new career? Was my livelihood going down the tubes along with my marriage? How was this all going to shake out? Did my choice in marrying what was turning out to be a very dangerous man negate my ability to be a pastor anymore? Not officially, I supposed, but I could see such poor choices in my personal life being held against me.

The first phone call I got at the church office began with, "So, I got your letter."

I held my breath, closed my eyes, and braced myself for what was coming next.

"I just wanted you to know, you will get through this. I promise."

My eyes flew open as I stuttered some sort of response that I don't even remember at this point. The woman on the other end of the line continued. "I had a pastor show up on my doorstep with a lawyer one time and told me, 'We're getting you out of this marriage.' So I know what it's like."

I let out a strangled sob and cried, "But, he's sitting in federal prison!"

She very calmly responded with, "Well, sometimes that happens."

I'm sorry, *what?*

I could barely believe what I was hearing. I made an immediate mental note that this woman and I really needed to talk further about her story.

I would continue to receive understanding from members of my congregation. Many women just started dropping by my office to share their stories with me.

If there's something this entire process would eventually teach me: there are a lot of women with stories that they rarely share with anyone. People you would have no idea what they endured in their marriages have stories. I was stunned by the number of women who were in dangerous, abusive situations and never left. They stayed with their abuser until the day their husband died.

What I came to realize was only when they feel you can understand where they've been will they open up to you and share their stories.

Out of tragedy come holy moments.

I would also start learning from several of my congregation members about some of my husband's shenanigans that had been going on around town without my knowledge. His anger issues had apparently become well-known. He'd thrown things at bank clerks, and had received numerous restraining orders from local businesses—including his own court-ordered counselor. I'm not sure how I was completely oblivious to these realities, but somehow I was. People apparently had been trying to protect me and not stress me out with this information. So I'd remained in the dark.

Even the senior pastor I worked with said his wife had concerns because she worked for the school system in Kearney, and they had received word from the school system in Omaha to watch out for him. I knew none of this until long after the fact.

My friends even came one afternoon to help me pack up everything of my husband's and put it in a storage unit that he had rented several months earlier following the flooding of my basement from a faulty water heater.

What we found when we began to go through all of his stuff was, to say the least, profoundly disturbing. I'd never thought much about some of the weapons he possessed—the crossbows, the throwing knives. But when we found a "secret" compartment in his dresser that I didn't know existed, we found a strange assortment of "toys" that were likely used for BDSM (Bondage, Domination, Sadism, Masochism) type of use. While the items had never been used on me (mainly because I refused to indulge certain suggestions he sometimes had in the bedroom), it begged the question: who had they been used on? You don't simply own those items on a whim. Whatever terrible sick and twisted things you might be thinking—I'll simply say, you're probably right. Those aren't my stories to tell, however. As I said—they wound up never being used on me.

But they were used.

Still, between the million-dollar life insurance policy and the strange assortment of both weapons and items that looked like they were straight out of *Fifty Shades of Grey*, an unsettling picture began to emerge regarding what plans he possibly had in mind for me further down the line. Compounded with the domestic violence history—connecting the dots wasn't hard. I had always been simply a means to an end for him. The federal court system just kept getting in the way.

My friends simply packaged everything up and got it out of my sight. They kept me focused, knowing that I was emotionally and mentally just spent. They knew I didn't at that time have the mental capacity to fully comprehend or process the items they uncovered. More than once they'd open a drawer, immediately close it and say I wasn't allowed to look inside.

They were the hands and feet of Christ. They were my saving grace.

Twelve
Moonlight Sonata

"The moon is a truer mirror for my soul than the sun that looks the same way every day."

— Barbara Brown Taylor, *Learning to Walk in the Dark*

FAIRY TALES HAVE INSPIRED a wide range of musical compositions. Tchaikovsky wrote his *Sleeping Beauty in the Woods* ballet in 1890 based on Charles Perrault's *Sleeping Beauty* story from 1697. Disney has long told its animated feature films as musicals. Perhaps this is because like visual art, music can communicate feelings, emotions, and atmospheres more directly than words and is able to make the unreal spring to life—making it the natural companion to imagination and fantasy as it helps enhance the magical or fantastical elements. The symbiotic relationship enhances the storytelling as the music helps engage the audience's imagination.

So it's really probably not a surprise that I also have a deep love of classical music. Piano playing, however, wound up not being my forté despite eight years of lessons. I finally gave up any delusions that I might one day be a concert pianist—not that I really ever thought that was a possibility—when I realized that my hands were too small to reach the more complicated chords that were required for the difficult pieces I wanted to play. Those same stubby fingers also lacked the fluid grace to dance across the keys in the rapid staccatos I yearned to master, instead invariably stumbling and bumbling over the keys in a muddled mess. Beethoven's "Pathetique" is still the bane of my existence.

I did continue to play the piano for many more years simply as a means of relaxation, and even owned a piano up until I went on seminary internship. I sadly had to leave it behind in Minnesota as I couldn't afford to have it moved anymore. I consequently fell out of practice and turned to my other hobbies—like painting—for relaxation. But I still have a love and appreciation for classical piano music, even if I can't really play it anymore.

Beautiful, comforting and relaxing, are the things I have always associated with piano music.

I remember the first Saturday evening I had to lead worship after I had informed the congregation of my impending divorce. I was nervous, afraid that I was going to fall apart in the middle of the service. Afraid someone was going to say something to me about how *dare* I get divorced. I had taken vows. It was my duty to stick by my husband.

I had every awful scenario I could think of running through my head. I wanted nothing more than to just go home and stick my head in the ground and never emerge again.

Yet as I made my way out of the sacristy and into the sanctuary that Saturday evening, the sounds of the prelude washed over me like a comforting wave, cradling me in its arms. I sat down, looked up at the cross that hung above the altar and felt a sense of peace I did not know was possible in that moment. A calm settled over me, and I led the worship service with a strange sense that things were going to be all right. Perhaps it was just getting back into the routines of doing what you know best that helps to calm us down, but I know the simple sound of church hymns brought me comfort in that moment.

Music carries a particular rhythm that can either excite us or relax us—carrying us away on the tides of melody.

The ocean, as well, has its own almost musical rhythm to it, and has always been a source of peace and comfort, despite the incident where I nearly drowned in the undertow. The experience did not drive me away from the ocean, however. It only made me respect undertows a bit more. I have always loved swimming and up until a year or two before my marriage, I swam regularly. Then, neck, back, and shoulder problems afflicted me, and doing the kind of swimming I was used to became impossible for a time, as the motion aggravated my injuries. While the backstroke was no longer possible, just floating in water actually had the opposite effect and alleviated the constant pain I was in. The release from gravity, the gently rolling waves, just made all the pain evaporate. Unfortunately, I couldn't live my life lying on my back in a pool of water—though it would be interesting to try.

Luckily, after several years of slowly working on swimming, I am now able to once again swim laps on a daily basis. I have returned to my "home," the water—that place of healing for me.

I don't know if my love of water has anything to do with the fact that it is a symbol of creation, chaos, and new life. A paradox of both comfort and fear.

I doubt I'm that self-aware, but who knows what goes on in that weird subconscious of mine. I just know there is something soothing and otherworldly about submerging under the waves and having the world around me muted, while at the same time mingled with a sense of danger and the unknown if one drifts too far.

Admittedly, I'm ready for the world to just not suck anymore. There has always been the presence of death and brokenness in my line of work. It seems even that our world as a whole has descended into a state of bizarre, surrealistic chaos of late.

But as I painted this, I felt the rhythms of the universe, felt the melody of new life and new beginnings taking shape. It seemed fitting as I started this painting to have both a sense of peace and chaos, that which I find comforting producing those images of new life. The things I find peaceful simultaneously erupting into a flurry of movement.

Butterflies have, of course, long been associated with renewal and rebirth—a symbol of transformation. A transformation so extreme that the end product no longer even remotely resembles the original caterpillar it evolved from. Yet despite such a dramatic transformation, it gracefully embraces change in its life.

I could feel the butterfly beckoning me to retain faith even when the tides of life were sweeping me in new directions. To lift my legs and ride the waves instead of fighting with futility against the deadly undertow beneath that threatened to pull me under and overwhelm me.

I wasn't there yet, but I felt as though I was going into a type of cocoon phase of life. The old me was gone. I didn't know what the new me was going to emerge like just yet. I was still in the midst of the transformation. I was still in the very early stages of fighting for my life, as it were.

Peacock feathers frame either side of this painting. The peacock has been utilized throughout history among many different religions, including Christianity, to symbolize immortality. The ancient Greeks believed that peacock flesh did not decay after death. Early Christian paintings and mosaics used peacock imagery, and peacock feathers were frequently displayed during

Easter services. The fact that the peacock sheds its feathers annually has always been a symbol of renewal and resurrection.

In Greek mythology, it is said the Goddess Hera placed eyes on the peacock's feathers, symbolizing the all-seeing knowledge and the wisdom of the heavens. It is also known among multiple, particularly Eastern, cultures as representing beauty, love, compassion, soul, peace and purity. Buddhist purification ceremonies have used peacock feathers for healing for over a thousand years. They are said to carry spiritual healing energy that can be used to assist people seeking balance and harmony in their lives.

I found myself drawn to these kinds of images because they're where I found my hope. I was so exhausted just battling every moment of every day, that these images found their way into my psyche. I needed healing for my body, mind and spirit.

As for the moon imagery, Barbara Brown Taylor said it best in her book, *Learning to Walk in the Dark*, "The moon is a truer mirror for my soul than the sun that looks the same way every day."

My hope when I created this was that it conveyed and expressed the vibrant explosion of healing and renewing life that emerges from the sonorous songs of life, riding out the waves with grace.

It was the hope I had. I was still "walking in the dark," but I was listening and watching and grasping for a life beyond the chaos.

Thirteen
Vortex of Crazy

> *"You think you're losing your mind, but do keep in mind, as long as you may, that the ability to go on thinking such a thing means it's not all gone."*
>
> — Criss Jami, *Killosophy*

MOST FAIRY TALES HAVE a villain. An evil stepmother. A crazed fashionista who likes to make clothing out of dogs. Rarely, if ever, is the villain masquerading as the Prince in an effort to drive the Princess insane. Villains are usually out there in the open and easy to identify. You don't fall in love with the villain in a fairy tale. The Prince doesn't try to destroy the life of the Princess. Even in the horrifying tale of the Robber Bridegroom, she never falls in love with him. She sees him for what he is and is able to escape the horrifying fate of marrying him.

Which is maybe why we are woefully unprepared with how to deal with discovering the person we love and adore is not only the villain in our story, but literally is the person in our orbit who does everything they can to destroy us.

Because when you rip the Prince Charming mask off the villain, you unlock a new level of hell.

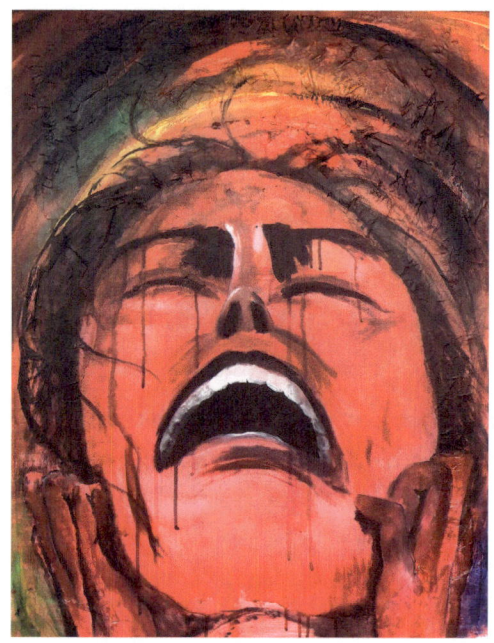

When you trigger narcissistic injury in a narcissist, you by default trigger rage. This occurs when their "true self" is unveiled, and they feel injury at being humiliated, rejected, or abandoned. Subsequently they feel threatened by this discovery and begin to lash out in dangerous and explosive outbursts that can morph into extreme acts of revenge.

Obviously, the moment I decided to file for divorce, I triggered this narcissistic injury and subsequent rage.

The only predictable part is that there will be some form of daily crazy that he throws at you. You won't have any idea what form the crazy will take, but you know the crazy is coming. Yet, no matter how prepared you are for the crazy to drop, it will still surprise you.

Because normal humans don't have brains that work the same way a narcissist's brain will work. No matter how hard you try to prepare and brace yourself for what's coming, you can never fully see it coming.

Even from prison, he was able to reach out and harass me. First, it came through his parents. He would use them to call or email me daily with some stupid little thing that he wanted or needed done. Eventually, I had to cut off communication with them and directed them to communicate only with my attorney going forward.

I soon realized this was the tactic I needed to take with all his friends and family, with the exception of his one brother who had already declared he preferred to lose my husband as his brother and keep me as his sister.

My husband's family was far from being free of his abusive tendencies.

Back when my husband was still on house arrest, he had shut off his daughter's phone while she was staying with her uncle. Angry, my brother-in-law had called and told him to release the account so he could at least pay for it because he didn't want his niece out there with him with no way to communicate with anyone. The two got into a fight.

My husband, in response to this fight, decided to hack into his brother's employer's website and outed him as gay. In small town Nebraska, this was a deadly game to be playing with someone who was not fully out about their sexual orientation. In response, his brother threatened to turn him into his probation officer, which only elicited another round of retaliation.

When I discovered what he'd done, I was beyond angry. But when I decided to sleep in a different room, I was told I was being disloyal for not taking his side in the argument. I was utterly appalled that he thought just because we were married that somehow meant I would endorse terrible behaviors.

Now I had gone and done the ultimate betrayal: I had filed for divorce. Not only did I file for divorce, but I did it while he was in a weakened position, sitting in a prison cell. The ultimate humiliation and limited ability to manipulate me due to the restraining order or do anything about it was maddening for him.

Still, he found ways to lash out, even from Leavenworth.

Sadly, he still had friends who were willing to be his enablers. As mentioned in an earlier chapter, I hadn't bothered to block his Facebook account because he was in prison and shouldn't have had access to social media. Still, the incident of me walking out of Red Lobster without paying my bill because of a surprise post that was designed to turn my congregation members against me was just the beginning of the chaos that would ensue over the next two years.

He began sending letters to my bishop, my council president, and the senior pastor I worked with. While my council president and the senior pastor handed me the letters they had received, unopened, I can only assume the bishop or someone on his staff must have read the one he received, as not long after this, the synod attorney sent a letter out to him telling him to cease and desist. (A synod is the local or provincial assembly of bishops and other church officials meeting to resolve questions of discipline or administration.) Upon his release from prison, he continued his harassment of the bishop's office and the synod attorney, to the point that the synod attorney sent out an email stating, *"If something would happen to me, I would follow up and check with [my husband's last name]. This is not someone to fool around with."*

He created a website that was for the sole purpose of telling the world what a horrible, awful person I was for divorcing him, going so far as to post my banking information for the world to see. I found out about that when a church member sent me the link. His daughter had shared it on her Facebook page and her daughter had seen it.

Essentially, given he could not communicate with me directly due to the protection order in place, he was going after everyone around me in the hopes that they would become so annoyed and afraid that they would abandon me, leaving me friendless and alone. He was attempting to isolate me—a task he'd never quite managed to accomplish while we were married.

He failed because my friends were the absolute best. My colleagues were, too, from the standpoint that they continued to show concern for me and my situation, clearly not listening to whatever accusations and lies he would throw my direction.

The barrage and demands that kept coming from him were seemingly endless. Even while we were in the midst of moving his stuff out of the house and into a storage unit, he had his parents call me to tell me I needed to stop with the removal of his property from the house.

We opted not to. We continued, and I eventually attained a judge's order that it was perfectly fine for me to remove his property from the house and put it into a storage unit.

While he was in prison, he sent me at least six multiple-page letters that went unread. Well, unread by me, at any rate. My best friend read them so I wouldn't have to, just to make sure they didn't contain any specific threats to my safety. When they were deemed to be something I really didn't need to bother reading, I eventually tore them all up and crumpled them onto a canvas that I then painted over with swirls of red and black with just a primal scream emitting from them. It was my vortex of crazy. It was a piece that was just raw emotion and pain. It was my ickiness spilled out on canvas. Even worse, it is made up of, literally, someone else's dark side and ickiness as well.

The process was cathartic and therapeutic if nothing else. And no, I will never know exactly what they contained. I don't need to. I'd read others he'd written, and these were allegedly worse, so there is nothing I care to ever see or know from them.

This piece was a reflection of how it felt to live my life at that time—that I had been sucked into this strange, terrible, and violent vortex that ripped everything in my world apart. It forced me to realize there was a side of life—and psychology—that I had never experienced before, but that millions of other women were facing on a daily basis. That life could be so twisted and, well, crazy, that you felt yourself spiraling out of control in a tornado-like swirl of emotional insanity.

It only got worse once he got out of prison.

I had warned the church office where I worked on multiple occasions that the first thing he was going to do when he got out was come to my home and office. For four months I begged that they install a security system. At home, my parents helped me get a home security system installed complete with cameras.

Two weeks out from his release date, Kearney had a night of severe storms and tornadoes. We watched with shock as the lower level of Good Samaritan Hospital flooded after the glass windows that kept the outside world, well, outside, shattered. It wouldn't be until the next day when I received a phone call from a parishioner informing me that the storage units where my husband's stuff was stored had been flooded as well.

Upon discovering this, I slid down the wall to the floor of my office and began laughing hysterically. Everything he owned had been destroyed in a flood. Naturally, I knew I would be blamed for this.

I wasn't wrong.

The stress eventually became such that I nearly blacked out one day in the office. I was standing in our youth pastor's doorway when I felt this strange dizzying wave wash over me and I nearly collapsed. Concerned, I went immediately to the doctor only to discover I was in hypertensive crisis: 176/114 was not a good blood pressure in case you're wondering. Given I had always had very low blood pressure, this was a shock to my system. I was immediately put on medication and almost hospitalized.

It's just wild what stress does to the body.

On August 13th, 2014, he was released from prison. I'd anticipated that his first stop when he got out of prison would be my place.

Again, I wasn't wrong.

I'd had the forethought to take that week off. My father was in Canada fishing, but I headed to Lincoln, and my mother and I were planning the next day to go to visit my brother and his family in Minneapolis. On my way to Lincoln, I received a panicked phone call from my senior pastor. My soon-to-be-ex had stopped by the church and confronted the senior pastor.

Apparently at some point the senior pastor had tried to show my husband out and placed a hand on his shoulder. My soon-to-be ex accused him of assault and marched down to the police station to file a complaint. The senior pastor wanted me to call the police and deal with him.

I laughed. "He didn't do this to me," I explained. "*You* have to report this—*you* have to deal with it. I tried to warn you."

The most frustrating part about being a woman is we are not taken seriously when we warn people about the threats we are facing. I spent four months warning the church staff what would happen. They brushed me off as overreacting.

Yet, when the senior pastor got a taste of what I had been experiencing on a regular basis, we had a security system in place in less than two weeks.

Given how quickly he showed up at the church, once I got to Lincoln, Mom and I decided not to wait until the next day to head to Minneapolis. As soon as I pulled into the driveway, we loaded Mom's stuff into the car and headed to Des Moines where we spent the night. Neither one of us put it past him coming out to my parents' place.

For the next week we stayed in Minneapolis with my brother, and I spent some time with friends.

As predicted, he began posting on social media how I had ruined all of his stuff, apparently by conjuring a flood. Because, of course, I had the power to control the weather. Seriously, if I possessed that kind of power, destroying his storage unit full of useless crap was not first on my list of things I would have done.

Eventually I had to return home, though I did have a home security system with video cameras that seemed to deter him from actually coming to the house. Along with the protection order a judge had granted me.

I have to also hand it to the Kearney police department. I could not step foot outside my house during my divorce without seeing a cop car somewhere in the three-block vicinity between the church and my home. While they couldn't officially monitor me twenty-four-seven, they were clearly aware enough of the danger he posed, not just to me but to others, that I couldn't go anywhere without knowing they were nearby. In fact, the friend who helped me go through all his paperwork stopped by my house one day before I got home and parked outside to wait for me. Not much more than a minute had gone by before the police were asking him who he was and what he was doing there. He said later he felt pretty good about my security.

I fully recognize, of course, the amount of privilege I possessed to receive that kind of treatment. Most women, when they report abuse, are first of all, not always believed. Second, rarely, if ever, is anyone looking out for them in the realm of law enforcement. My status as a faith leader in the community granted me these privileges, and that has never been lost on me. I grapple with being extremely grateful for that kind of protection—and also deeply disturbed by how such scenarios go for so many other women who do not have my same privileged status in society.

Protection orders and a constant police presence didn't stop him from harassing the people around me, however. He showed up one day at the campus ministries where my best friend was the pastor. Neither of us were there, but apparently he had begun trying to develop a romantic relationship with one of the college students. There are absolutely no words to describe the amount of disgust and shame and fear I felt upon learning this. I couldn't help feeling it was my fault that some college student was being subjected to his harassment. I was the one who had introduced him to the world of campus ministries and given him access to vulnerable female students. His proclivity for younger girls would soon become more apparent, and all it ever leaves me with is just a profound sense of revulsion that has sickened me to my core.

I should have seen it, though. I should have known when he came to me one day during our marriage, and he asked if he should let his seventeen-year-old daughter pose for a sexually explicit calendar and poster. I told him absolutely not. A seventeen-year-old should not be subjected to that type of exploitation.

He ignored me and took her to the photo shoot. His daughter would later tell me that she had never wanted to do the photo shoot, but he had pushed her into it and had spent the entire time on the set ogling all the other girls. He'd always framed it as something she wanted to do, and it was just a question of whether or not he allowed her to do it. Lies upon lies.

A divorce that should have taken six months wound up taking two years. Like with all his federal nonsense, he pulled stunts during the divorce that were just insane. One of the main playbooks of a narcissist in court is to accuse the judge of bias, misconduct, etc.

Divorce court was no different.

The first judge he accused of a conflict of interest because he happened to have the same last name as one of my parishioners. During that hearing, my lawyer and I sat in court with the judge as my husband was on the phone from wherever he was living in Omaha. He informed the judge he had filed some sort of formal complaint against him. At that point the judge stated he had no choice but to withdraw from the case and assign it to a new judge. Then he hung up the phone. Or thought he did.

For a moment we all sat there in silence. Then suddenly, my husband's voice came through the intercom.

"Are you still there? Hello?"

The judge raised a finger to his lips, indicating his desire for us to all stay silent and make him think we were not there anymore. I admit, the scene caused me to stifle a giggle. The whole scenario was utterly surreal and ridiculous.

Finally, we heard the click as the line disconnected for real this time. The judge just shook his head in disbelief as my lawyer walked over to the court clerk to get our case assigned to a new judge. I remained sitting behind the table as the judge stood and climbed down from where he sat. As he passed by where I was sitting, he paused, looked at me and said, "I'm so very sorry," and continued out of the courtroom. My attorney, witnessing this transaction, hurried over to me.

"Did the judge talk to you?"

I nodded. "Yeah."

He turned to look at the door where the judge exited then shook his head in amazement. "Judges don't do that. Ever," he said finally.

Those were hardly his final shenanigans. During the course of the divorce process he went through three different attorneys, the second of which showed up in court one day and requested to withdraw. When the judge questioned this, he simply responded with "you can either grant my withdrawal or disbar me. But one way or another I will not represent this person."

My attorney afterward informed me that in all his years of practicing law, he had never heard another attorney tell a judge to disbar him rather than represent a client.

My soon-to-be-ex-husband was always breaking unprecedented ground.

Like most narcissists, he always thought he was smarter than the attorneys. So for a while he represented himself.

I, too, wound up going through two different attorneys, but for different reasons. I started out with a female lawyer. A few months into the process, she informed me she would be handing my case off to one of her partners. She was pregnant, and her doctor had advised she not deal with my case. The doctor was aware of who my husband was—the joys of a small town—and advised her not to deal with that kind of toxic stress.

Yes. My husband was so toxic he could potentially cause a miscarriage. That's the kind of crazy we were dealing with.

After all, she had already experienced some of the crazy by this time. I remember an email she had sent to his first attorney stating that under no uncertain terms was my husband to ever come to their offices. He had been demanding to talk to them directly about the divorce case. After being hung up on a few times, he left a voicemail stating he was coming by the office. My attorney's email read:

> *"Please advise your client not to come to this office. I will not speak with him or discuss this case with him. In the event he ignores your advice and decides to show up we will have no choice but to phone the police. Your immediate attention with this is greatly appreciated. In the event you withdraw, as [he] keeps telling my staff, please advise him we will not discuss this case over the phone with him, but will only accept written correspondence from him regarding this matter."*

After her legal partner took over, the crazy only got worse. My ex's insanity was met with equal parts humor and disdain by my new, more "bulldog" style attorney.

My new lawyer would send responses like:

> *"King of the World: Enjoy the Looney Toones at your babysitting job."*

"What in the world are you talking about? I am not present at the conference calls you are apparently having with the council of elders on the planet Zoltron where you are apparently coming up with this stuff."

More of that twisted reality he lived in and tried to convince others existed.

My ex also continued to try and escalate issues with the synod and church office, accusing the senior pastor of a "brutal assault" (which, if you knew the senior pastor, you'd know how insane this claim was). Additionally, he was trying to get reimbursed for all of his volunteer hours at the church, demanding thousands of dollars in compensation, and demanded that I be banned from the church where I was a pastor. His argument was I had lied during our wedding when I vowed to stay married to him until death parted us. Therefore, I was a liar and should no longer be a pastor.

I mean if we want to talk about lies that were told during those wedding vows: love, honor and cherish were pretty big ones.

The synod attorney sent an email out, discussing my husband's latest "missile," and then stated, "You mentioned the fact that his anger would escalate. The way I read the most recent email, it has escalated."

Then of course there was the accusation that I married him "fraudulently," by claiming I wanted children and then went on birth control to prevent that from happening. He thus tried to sue me for fraud.

I'm not sure what I found more insulting: the fact that he attempted this in the first place, or that my attorney had the audacity to ask me if it was true.

I'm sorry, what kind of question is that exactly?

Reality was I absolutely did want children. But when your husband gets arrested by federal marshals seven months into your marriage and winds up coming home on house arrest, you begin to re-evaluate these choices. So yes, I went back on birth control because I didn't want to bring a child into the insanity that was our lives at the time.

The truly unfortunate part, however, is that I was not the only one suffering a traumatic experience due to my husband.

One day, when we heard he was coming to Kearney, I called my best friend, the campus pastor. She was standing in the lobby of her therapist's office when I called, and when she got off the phone, the receptionist behind the counter went pale and asked if it was my husband who was coming to town. When my friend answered yes, the girl burst into tears and asked to take the rest of the afternoon off from work.

Apparently, she'd experienced his narcissistic rage first-hand at some point as well. Which wasn't surprising as it was the same office that had done his court-ordered diagnosis and therapy that he thought was all wrong and biased. He'd tried to demand they pay him a million dollars in damages. Oh yes, the demanding people pay him exorbitant amounts of money when they upset him was a fun trademark of his. I found multiple copies of letters demanding these kinds of things from all sorts of different people he felt had wronged him for one reason or another.

When the time came for me to sell my home, I warned the real estate agent that I had a crazy soon-to-be ex-husband, so be prepared, and I totally understood if he didn't want to deal with that nonsense. He waved his hand dismissively.

"Oh, I've dealt with crazy exes before," he laughed.

I gave him a skeptical look and went, "I don't think you've experienced this kind of crazy before."

Still, he seemed unconcerned, and I decided that I'd tried to warn him, that was the best I could do.

It didn't take long for me to start receiving frantic phone calls and texts from my realtor wanting me to call the police because my ex-husband was completely unhinged and had started threatening him. Not only that, my ex had taken to posting in the Facebook Kearney Exchange page about what a terrible real estate agent he was because he was unlawfully trying to sell a home that he had no right to sell. This would affect his reputation and his business, so he was frantic. But it was the threats to show up at his house that I think truly terrified him.

I had to sigh. Saying, "I tried to warn you," didn't seem like the best response, but...I'd tried to warn him. I informed him the threats were not being directed at me, therefore, there was nothing I could do about it. If he wanted to call the police, he'd have to call the police himself.

I absolutely hated that his destructive and psychotic behavior was spilling out and affecting everyone around me. But that's what they do. It's how they know they can get to you—when they aren't allowed to come after you directly. They simply go after everyone around you instead, hoping that they'll be so upset that you brought this terror into their lives that they want nothing more to do with you and therefore ditch you personally or professionally. That was, no doubt, his goal. To create this vortex of crazy that everything and everyone around me got swept up into.

My parents were swept up in the vortex as well. At one point, he thought they were helping me financially to pay for the divorce attorneys (they weren't), so he called them and began threatening to freeze all of their financial assets unless they stopped helping me. Because, he clearly had that kind of power and ability.

My parents immediately called the police, and they made a visit to him that seemed to end his attempts to harass my parents directly. I believe the police officer's response to the recording was something to the effect of, "Some people are simply a waste of oxygen."

While I have since moved on from all of the anxiety and fear that once dominated my life, I still feel the effects sometimes of the swirling madness. Of there being no control whatsoever in my life. Of my reality shattering and being swept into what hell must be very similar to.

When I hear other women's stories, it can bring me back to that time, and I ache for them. Because I know that while you're going through it, you do not see the light at the end of the tunnel. People keep telling you there is one, but it's not visible at the moment, so it's hard to believe it actually exists. Because the attacks that are coming at you are so bizarre, so vicious, and so random—that you are constantly on guard and always off-balance. That it will only take one. more. thing. to tip you into that soul-sucking insanity that finally does you in.

Yet, somehow, you survive. You're not sure how. You're not sure why. You're not sure how you held life together by the small threads you were clinging to. Yet you did. Somehow you survived the vortex of crazy.

Fourteen
The Maelstrom

"I don't feel calm at all. I am a maelstrom of emotions. All I want to do is scream."

—— Holly Black, *The Queen of Nothing*

DISNEY'S *MAELSTROM* RIDE WAS eventually replaced by *Frozen Ever After*. For those who remember it, it was a lovely little Norwegian ride on a Viking longboat, until you met the trolls that cursed you and sent you shooting backwards, then turned the boats around so they plunged forward down a twenty-eight-foot flume into a stormy depiction of the North Sea. After passing very close to an oil rig, the ride came to an abrupt end in a calm harbor of a small village. It was that mixture of serenity and beauty suddenly upended by chaos and upheaval.

Cursed by a troll. Well, that was certainly one way to look at it.

A maelstrom is, by definition, a situation or state of confused movement or violent turmoil. As much as I sought calm in my life, I knew I would never find it as long as the divorce proceedings were going on.

When I'd first met with my initial attorney, she thought it would cost about three thousand dollars and a few months to go through the process. She had absolutely no idea what we were in for, and I didn't even know how to prepare her for it because I had no idea how he ultimately would respond. I had not yet seen the full brunt of his narcissism, so I was just as woefully unprepared for the barrage of insanity that would eventually follow.

Our first offer included him getting most of the marital assets acquired during the marriage along with three thousand dollars in cash. There was no more money left in my savings, and he was swimming in credit card debt. Between the wedding and paying for multiple attorneys for his federal court hearings, we'd completely wiped out any savings I had before we got married. In fact, I'd had to borrow money from a colleague to pay off one of the attorney bills, and my parents had given us a loan for the car we'd bought together when he realized he needed to lower his car payments. So our combined assets were minimal, with only household items to argue and fight over. Which honestly, I'd have let him have everything except the house and the dog if it meant getting it over with faster, but my attorney refused to let me do that.

Thankfully, he had no claim to the house—it was mine from before we met, and I had never put his name on it like he'd wanted me to. His real goal was of course to go after my pension that I had through the church, to siphon off as much as he could from my retirement. Given the short amount of time we were married, however, he was only entitled to half of whatever it had gained between the date of our marriage and the date I filed for divorce, which only amounted to two and a half years.

Naturally, he threw the offer back in our faces and demanded I pay him over a hundred thousand dollars. My attorney and I actually laughed out loud, and I think that was the moment she began to realize what we were dealing with.

There would be no reasoning. There would be no good-faith negotiation.

When he got out of prison, he wanted in the house to go through everything that was there. I was nervous about letting him in, and obviously he couldn't be allowed to go through it alone. By then I'd been handed over to the bulldog attorney, so I wound up paying him to babysit my soon-to-be-ex while he went through house listing his assets.

What he turned in to the court was such a ridiculous asset list that I honestly was utterly confused and disoriented as to what to do with it. He'd listed my artwork as being worth over thirty million dollars (good night, don't I wish!), and in an effort to embarrass me listed not only all the strange sexual paraphernalia we'd discovered in his dresser, but added a variety of other sexual toys and items just for good measure.

My attorney was livid, immediately recognizing what he was doing. Unfortunately for my ex, I did not embarrass easily, and I replied with, "For thirty million dollars, the value he's assigned to my paintings, he can literally have everything."

By the time our court date rolled around in May of 2015—which had been postponed and rescheduled for over a year now—he'd managed to bring that figure down to something more reasonable, like thirty thousand, which was still ridiculously high.

Regardless, he had secured his third attorney by the time we made our way into the court room for the actual hearing. As expected, it was filled with more nonsense and craziness. At one point, while he was on the stand, he started referencing some of the messages my attorney had sent him when he'd not had legal counsel of his own, in particular the email asking him what planet he was from.

Admittedly, neither my attorney nor I could help ourselves. We both snickered a little from behind our table.

His head snapped angrily in our direction before he turned to the judge and demanded a ten minute recess. My attorney leaned over and went, "Clients don't get to demand recesses from judges."

However, this particular judge was also fighting back the giggles apparently and granted the recess, quickly jumping up and disappearing into his chambers, to no doubt laugh and marvel at the absurdity of it all. I have no doubt judges see a lot of antics in their courtrooms. Still, some things have to take even them by surprise.

My ex stalked out of the courtroom, leaving his attorney to stand there, shaking his head and muttering, "The longer this takes the more it's going to cost him."

Eventually he returned, and the proceedings resumed rather uneventfully from that point forward. When we broke for lunch, he and my dad apparently had a run-in inside the men's bathroom. Not sure on what planet, (Voltron, perhaps?) after sending my parents threatening messages, he thought trying to strike up some idle chit-chat with my father was a good idea, but he tried anyway. He asked if my dad planned on going moose hunting in Colorado that fall.

My dad, ever the diplomat, simply said, "Oh, don't worry. I'll shoot something."

With the court hearing finally out of the way, I breathed a sigh of relief. Surely the end was in sight, right? Like it would take the judge maybe six weeks to make his ruling?

What I didn't count on were the judge's plans to retire at the end of the year. He knew my ex-husband's history of challenging and appealing any court decision that didn't go his way. So he sat on our case. For months. In fact, during that time, I discovered my senior pastor was taking a new call, forcing me to take a new call, and by the time the ruling came down, I was living over seventeen hundred miles away.

Which of course complicated issues because it meant I'd had to move everything when I sold the house. Whatever he got in the divorce, I'd have to send back.

In December of 2015 the judge finally issued his ruling, right before he retired so that when my ex filed his inevitable appeal and began screaming about how corrupt and unfair it was (he got absolutely no money, and the judge had pretty well split all the household assets in half—and denied him the alimony he was seeking) the judge simply didn't respond to his threats to take it all the way to U.S. Supreme Court. Which, you know, isn't a thing for a civil divorce case.

By now, I knew exactly what was going to happen when I shipped back all the things that he was being given in the divorce—he was going to claim I destroyed and broke it all before sending it back. I carefully wrapped everything in bubble wrap, took photos of it wrapped in bubble wrap in the plastic bins that I then hired movers to take and deliver to his parents, since he still did not have an address of his own. I spent over three thousand dollars shipping back a sofa-sectional, the recliner, and a few other large items along with the glassware from our wedding.

As predicted, his attorney sent my attorney a scathing email claiming everything arrived broken and destroyed. I had the pictures to prove that everything went on the moving truck in one piece and well-wrapped. If they got destroyed, take it up with the moving company.

Finally, the thirty-day time to file an appeal expired, and on January 4th, 2016, I was finally, legally, free. Sadly, I was now living in another state and had no one to go out and celebrate my new-found freedom with.

Still, it was at least one chapter that was finally over. One element of the crazy that had been resolved. I was finding some sense of calm in the midst of the whirlwind.

Even once order had been established, an element of chaos continued to exist. My "Maelstrom" painting was meant to signify how the energy we put into our lives and relationships is sometimes carefully controlled—and other times spiders out in unexpected streams. Sometimes life seems like it is being directed somewhere —and other times it seems to be spiraling out of control into a vortex of swirling winds and water.

Life. Creation. Chaos. Order. Energy. Power. Resurrection. New life. "The Maelstrom" of life. Because even though the divorce was now final—it wasn't fully and completely the end.

Narcissists never let it be the end.

Fifteen
Into the Wilderness

"To be whole. To be complete. Wilderness reminds us what it means to be human, what we are connected to rather than what we are separate from."

— Terry Tempest Williams

CHARACTERS IN FAIRY TALES are often driven from their homes and out into the wilderness. The Huntsman in *Snow White* takes her into the woods and tells her to run and escape. Princess Aurora in *Sleeping Beauty* is raised in the woods by her three fairy godmothers. *Hansel and Gretel* are dropped off in the woods and have to try to find their way back home.

Wilderness metaphors are always portrayed as a time of danger and searching.

Likewise, in the Bible the wilderness is a place of temptation, trial, testing, and training. A place of danger and chaos. It's a place where ordinary life is suspended. A place of isolation and uncertainty. A place of risk.

Yet also a place to experience God.

Israel spent forty years in the wilderness after their deliverance from Egypt as they had proven time and again they were not ready to be God's people with their grumbling, complaining, challenging, and unfaithfulness. Still, God remained with them throughout the journey (with Moses having to talk God out of just striking them all dead out of frustration a few times). It was a place where they confronted fear, thirst, hunger, and adversity. It was where their mettle was tested, where they were shaped and formed. Where they learned to trust in God.

Jesus spent forty days in the wilderness fasting until he was weakened and then tested and tempted to succumb to worldly power and self-sufficiency. He was tempted to wield the power of God for his own benefit rather than relying on the sufficiency of God. He ultimately succeeded where Israel had previously fallen short.

In both cases, it was a time of struggle and identity. Discerning who and what they were. Finding out through adversity what they were truly made of.

I likewise faced my own wildernesses in life. My times of struggle and adversity, when I felt isolated and abandoned. But if I didn't move forward and plunge headlong into the unknown deserts of life, allowing myself to be molded and shaped by life's challenges—I risked being overcome by the world when it cracked around me, falling into a chasm of despair and regret that I could not climb my way out of. I could not be paralyzed by the past but rather I had to move into the future—as daunting and barren as it seemed at times.

My wildernesses were where I, too, like the ancient Israelites, discovered who and what I was. It felt as though life was cracking open beneath my feet and threatening to swallow me whole. Pushing me forward into desolate and unknown wildernesses.

I've experienced many wilderness moments in my life. It seems I'm frequently facing struggle and testing. Even when I attended seminary, I saw that as a "wilderness" experience. I used to state that God was like a soccer mom who forgot to come back and get her kid. It felt at times like God had called me to this whole ministry thing, led me to seminary, then kind of dropped me off and forgot about me. It was a time of intense spiritual struggle as my faith was challenged, torn down, and then eventually built back up. As I already described in an earlier chapter, seminary created some pretty seismic shifts in my faith journey and worldview. It pushed me to discover whether this was truly my calling or not.

My divorce was most definitely yet another time of wilderness wandering for me. I was forced to discover what I was made of. My resilience, my ability to grow and forge forward in life despite all the trauma I was struggling to recover from.

There were huge cracks in the ground that threatened to swallow me whole at times. I always felt I was trying to keep just one step ahead of complete and utter disaster.

My mother, on more than one occasion, had commented she didn't know how I survived the things I did, that she would not have. Well, no one knows what they're capable of surviving until they have to go through them.

You survive because you have to. You have no other choice except to die, and that was not really an option in my world. That doesn't mean I was not injured and scarred by the experience.

I was fearful as I progressed in my therapy that my brain might be irretrievably changed by everything I was going through. I was suffering from memory issues and had trouble concentrating on things the way I once had. I was learning that trauma does this to the brain.

Emotional trauma and post traumatic stress disorder (PTSD) do cause both brain and physical damage. Neuropathologists have seen overlapping effects of physical and emotional trauma upon the brain. With such an overlap it can be seen that both of these traumas have a detrimental effect upon the amygdala, the hippocampus and the prefrontal cortex of the brain, which essentially means that emotional trauma or PTSD does indeed result in brain injury/damage.

Dr. Todd Thatcher writes:

> *"These three parts of the brain—the amygdala, the hippocampus, and the prefrontal cortex—are the most-affected areas of the brain from trauma.*
>
> *They can make a trauma survivor constantly fearful, especially when triggered by events and situations that remind them of their past trauma."*[1]

My entire personality had changed during both my marriage and subsequent divorce. I was not aware I was being emotionally abused and manipulated, but my brain subconsciously was. After I filed for divorce and the narcissistic rage and abuse intensified, my "fight or flight" mode was in high gear. Walking into the grocery store was a challenge, and I'd started having panic attacks when in other public social settings.

---

1. Thatcher, Todd. "How Trauma Affects The Brain," highlandspringsclinic.org, February 2019

The fight or flight response is an automatic physiological reaction to an event that is perceived as stressful or frightening. The perception of threat activates the sympathetic nervous system and triggers an acute stress response that prepares the body to fight or flee.

I was in my early forties. I'd never had panic attacks or anxiety in my life. Now, I could barely function when I found myself in large groups of people. Which, as a pastor, you can imagine might be problematic.

Shortly after my husband had been arrested, I went to his cousin's graduation gathering at a restaurant. She was only slightly older than my step-daughter and she had spent a summer with us a year or so earlier. I liked her, so despite everything that was going on, I wanted to wish her well.

I was unable to stay for more than a few minutes before I began to feel like the walls were closing in on me. I had this panicked need to escape. Did any of them know what had been going on? I knew the cousin did. Who else did? It felt like people were staring at me. They knew. They were judging.

Panic seized me and I ran.

I made the mistake of thinking that going to the grocery store next would calm me down somehow.

Instead, I walked in, and completely froze. The mere thought of having to make a decision about what I was going to buy to eat was too much for my brain to process. So I grabbed a hunk of cheese from the deli, paid for it, and sped home.

I began to worry that my brain was going to be "stuck" in this reality for the rest of my life, that I'd never recover from the ways in which my life had shattered all around me. That I'd never go back to being who I was before I had met and married him.

In many ways, I was correct. I am not the same person. But then, no one is the same person they were ten years ago. I did suffer some permanent memory loss. There are things I simply cannot remember anymore from that time period. Things that I probably should have remembered. I thankfully wrote down a lot of what went on, and held on to paperwork which is how I was able to write much of this book. Writing from my emotions at the time was impossible, but I did have the presence of mind to record facts and details of things that were happening at the time in my journals. Not necessarily feelings, but just a record of what had transpired.

My art was where my feelings were expressed.

I found that I also had a lot of startle responses to people walking in on me unexpectedly.

I remember a few weeks after I started a new call, after I'd moved seventeen hundred miles away from where my ex lived, that someone walked into my office via an outside door that had been left unlocked.

I was so shaken by the incident that my anxiety rendered me completely paralyzed, and I had to go home for the rest of the afternoon.

There were times I didn't think I would ever move forward. That I was going to be stuck out in this wilderness. It didn't help matters that the senior pastor I'd been working with in Nebraska decided to take a new call mid-way through the divorce process. I was coterminous, which meant I was going to have to look for a new call as well.

In the denomination to which I belong, most synods made their associate pastors sign a coterminous agreement, meaning we had to leave our call when the senior pastor resigned their call. This was so associates could not try and undermine a senior pastor in order to try and take their position. The logic makes sense, but at that time in my life, leaving my support network was yet another blow to my psyche.

They say one of the worst things you can do during or up to one year after a divorce is move, change jobs, or uproot your life.

I wasn't even through my divorce process yet when I was forced to do all that and inadvertently walked into yet another abusive situation.

I also can't really express what it felt like to essentially be told by my synod that my leaving the state would be best. There's a part of me that knows they were trying to protect me. Given my skillset, the most likely move would have been to Omaha or Lincoln. Except, my ex-husband was living in the Omaha area, and Lincoln was only a mere forty-five-minute drive away. So my bishop didn't hesitate to release my mobility paperwork to other synods and told me they were not going to place me in Nebraska.

The other part of me felt like they were trying to get rid of me and send me far, far away not for my sake—but for their own. My leaving the synod would hopefully mean they would no longer have to deal with his nonsense anymore, either. It's not like they had been mere bystanders. The bishop and synod attorney had both been targets of his threats and craziness. So I couldn't help but feel a bit like they wanted to get me far away so that I'd take the craziness with me.

I also didn't really blame them. I wanted the craziness gone as much as they did.

Leaving the Nebraska Synod meant leaving my home, my family, my friends, and all the security of the people who had been looking out for me the past year or so.

It literally felt like the earth was cracking beneath me. Even as I ran to keep ahead of the chasm that was chasing me, threatening to drag me into the abyss of darkness and despair, it was like rocks were being thrown in my path to trip me up. The urge to literally just lie down and die, much like the prophet Elijah tried to do in the wilderness when he was fleeing Queen Jezebel after he killed her Baal prophets, was strong.

Yet, I didn't. I kept moving. I kept pushing forward.

My finances were wiped out, and when I sold my house, all the proceeds went toward paying off my thirty-thousand-dollar divorce attorney fees. I once again moved into an apartment, unable to afford a down payment for a home, and felt like I was having to start my life all over again—broke and broken, and seventeen hundred miles away from friends, family, and a local police department that knew and understood the danger I was in.

Once the divorce was finalized, I suddenly didn't hear from him anymore. I was a discarded toy that he could no longer get anything out of.

Except, despite the sudden silence, I didn't ever quite feel like it was over. That he was just biding his time.

A little over a year later, I received a message from a friend of his in Omaha asking me if I was okay. Confused I responded that yes, I was fine. She was relieved. She was worried that when she heard my ex-husband had moved to within three hours of where I was now living, that he was coming after me.

My anxiety level surged through the roof. Once again, he was now living only a mere three hours away. My attorney had once suggested that I change my name and develop a whole new identity. That was easier said than done, of course, especially given my public presence as a pastor, but the idea suddenly had a lot of merit. Was I going to spend the rest of my life running while he kept chasing after me? Were his intentions to kill me, or just keep harassing me and making my life a living hell once again? Investing in moving my security system to my new residence no longer seemed like an overreaction.

Only this time, I was alone. I didn't have my friends and family around to watch out for me. I didn't have a local police department that was very well-versed in how dangerous and unstable he was. My congregation was oblivious to the hell he'd put me through. My hyper-vigilance kicked back into high gear.

He didn't contact me after he moved, but I did learn about some of the antics and trouble he found himself in over in his new city and state. It apparently kept him busy enough not to mess with me.

But this time period utterly changed my faith in pretty seismic ways. I began to see life from a very different perspective. There was an awareness to how rapidly someone's life can change through no real fault of their own. I had to realize I had resources other women didn't. The "why doesn't she just leave" question irritates me to no end. Most don't leave because they don't have the support or the resources to leave.

I began to really think about the precarious position so many women find themselves in within a society that can be brutal and harsh if you don't have the finances to keep yourself afloat. I became more empathetic toward single mothers, people living in poverty, and the homeless.

My faith morphed from "Jesus saves us from hell," to a much more here and now lived reality. Hell is not just in the afterlife. It can be in the present. I began seeing how Jesus walked with, reached out to, and provided healing to those who society had dealt harshly with because life did not cut them any breaks.

I saw my own situation as being nothing compared to what others have had to face, and I gained a new appreciation for the will to survive and get through whatever the next thing is.

As much as I'd like to say my new state and new call became my haven, that soon turned out to not be the case. My new-found awareness for red flags of narcissism had made me extremely sensitive to those behaviors, and I soon discovered there are far more narcissists in our lives than we probably ever realize. I likely could not have pin-pointed the issues I was dealing with as rapidly—or at all—had I not gone through what I did with my ex-husband.

As the saying goes: out of the frying pan and into the fire. I had not escaped Wonderland quite as fully as I had hoped.

Sixteen
Games with No Rules

> *"If you don't know where you are going,
> any road can take you there."*
>
> — Cheshire Cat, *Alice in Wonderland*

ALICE DISCOVERS WHILE SHE'S in Wonderland that she's playing a game she doesn't know all the rules to, and doesn't know who her friends are, and who is trying to lead her down wrong paths. In addition to misdirection, the role of the Cheshire Cat was to use faulty logic and do whatever it could to frustrate Alice. To gaslight her and make her question her own sanity. Did she really experience what she thought she had?

The Cheshire Cat may have led her to her ultimate destination, but that wasn't before it spent a lot of time toying with Alice, and was clearly the "spiritual" essence of the madness that made up Wonderland. It did not help make sense of the madness, or guide her through the madness, but was in fact a willing participant in and product of the madness.

It constantly looked over her shoulder—sometimes seen, sometimes unseen. But always grinning that maddeningly smug grin that never allowed her to totally see what was going on or what it was doing.

It was there to remind her that it hadn't gone away and was still lurking in the darkness, just beyond sight, threatening to pop out of nowhere and once again try to derail her from reaching her destination of wholeness and happiness.

As my divorce neared its conclusion, I did not anticipate that I was going to escape one puppet master, only to find myself in the crosshairs of yet another one. The Joker from both *"The Puppet Master,"* and *"Down a Rabbit Hole"* in this painting transformed into the Cheshire Cat, a mischievous character who excelled in the art of misdirection, trying to throw Alice off course on more than one occasion.

Forces beyond my control had moved me to need to seek a new call, leaving behind my friends, family and support system. While I wasn't happy about the changing situation, I chose to approach it as an opportunity to start over. To have a new life that was geographically far away from the clutches of the insanity that had plagued my life for the past several years. To find a place that would allow me to heal.

This new, seeming paradise was supposed to be my haven. My "destination of wholeness and happiness." A place to recover and rest as I forged a new path and life for myself.

I escaped from the manipulative games I'd been tied up in with my husband, dove into the stormy seas of uncertainty in order to escape his dangerous fantasy world, only to arrive at my destination beaten and broken.

What I needed was respite.

To my dismay, what I found was I'd simply landed in another realm of Wonderland. I did not have a chance to even catch my breath before I realized that rather than finding the gentle caresses of the ocean carrying me to new life, I was in a tumultuous sea of chaos and gaslighting all over again.

Nearly drowned and still gasping for air, I rapidly discovered my place of respite had been a huge misdirection. I was still a pawn in someone else's game. I still had to walk on eggshells, trying to figure out all the changing expectations from day to day.

My divorce was not yet final, so I was still dealing with my ex-husband's nonsense. I now also had to deal with a whole new situation that nearly finished me off in a way my husband had not been able to; mainly because this time, it wasn't a singular individual who fed into the problem. It was a system.

It's not an accident that several of my paintings that deal with this topic of abuse and control utilize *Alice in Wonderland* imagery. Feminist scholars throughout the years have seen Alice as a complex female character who is both strong and assertive, an "underground image of a woman resisting the system," and yet is also subject to the male powers that surround her.[1] For instance, when the caterpillar tells her she "must eat" the mushroom, but doesn't tell her which side will do which, she is forced into a situation where she is denied the necessary information she needs in order to make an informed decision and thus does not have any control over what she consumes and the changes her body undertakes as a result of this eating.[2]

When I got married, I clearly didn't have all the information about who he was to make an informed decision. It was revealed piecemeal, and far too late. As I attempted to create a new life for myself, I rapidly discovered I had once

---

1. Little, Judith. "Liberated Alice: Dodgson's female hero as domestic rebel." Women's Studies 3.2 (1976): 195. Academic Search Premier. EBSCO. Web. 16 Feb. 2011.

2. Garland, Carina. "Curious Appetites: Food, Desire, Gender and Subjectivity in Lewis Carroll's Alice Texts." The Lion and the Unicorn 32.1 (2008): 22-39. Project MUSE. Web. 21 Jan. 2011

again been denied important information that I needed to make decisions that would have been for my own health and well-being in terms of my job. It was like playing a game without knowing all the rules.

Despite months of interviewing and going through the call process with a new congregation, the day after I signed the paperwork and informed my current congregation I was leaving, I received a phone call from the new synod I was going into. They wanted to inform me that it had been brought to their attention they had forgotten to mention some pretty critical information. Had I received that information sooner, I likely would have never even considered interviewing, much less signing on the dotted line.

Needless to say, that revelation stopped me dead in my tracks.

They'd just...*forgotten?*

The synod was quick to assure me that everything really was fine, that the information I viewed as alarming, and definitely a red flag, had no real merit and really was a non-issue, which is why they'd forgotten to mention it. Due to the confidential nature of the information they shared with me, I'm unfortunately not at liberty to divulge it publicly more than to simply say: it was bad.

I felt trapped. I couldn't go back to the congregation I'd just told I was leaving and go, "never mind, false alarm!" Once you let a congregation know you're leaving, you're a completely ineffective leader. I told myself surely the synod would not send me into a potentially harmful situation. They were well aware of what I'd just been through. I opted to trust their judgment. Given my modus operandi regarding giving people chances beyond when I should, I went forward with the call and moved.

Once again, I should have listened to my instinct. Despite how trapped in the situation I may have felt, I should have backed out and simply been an ineffective leader for a while. That would have been the wise thing to do.

I think I've proven, I'm not always wise. Hindsight is always twenty-twenty. I tried to tell myself that the situation deserved the benefit of the doubt. Yet, I came into it already tentative and hypervigilant. Not the best way to begin a new call.

I want to say that once I arrived, nothing at all seemed amiss. I *want* to say that. I want to say that I was able to jump in with both feet into this new life I was hoping I was going to create.

It would not be the truth, however.

It was only my second Sunday helping lead worship when my PTSD was triggered. Though honestly, it was more like "acute" rather than "post" traumatic stress as I was still dealing with the final vestiges of my divorce proceedings. My ex was still lashing out at me in whatever ways he could.

We were serving communion and apparently I wasn't standing where the senior pastor wanted me to be. So rather than simply point to where I should be standing, he came up behind me, grabbed both my arms tightly and physically shoved me to the area of the chancel he wanted me to stand.

It was like an anxiety spike shot through my brain and my hands began shaking so bad I could barely hold the chalice. I forced myself to finish the service, though it took tremendous effort. I tried to be aware of my own hypersensitivities, gritted my teeth and told myself I was making more out of it than was actually there. After all, it wasn't his fault I had trauma triggers.

Also—don't touch me. And certainly don't shove me around. No woman likes that.

As the weeks progressed, things didn't get a whole lot better. I think the senior pastor believed I was still an intern, rather than a pastor with nearly seven years of experience behind me, and tried to "help me out" by giving me advice on how I just needed to "be myself" around the congregation. I smiled and accepted the advice, as condescending as it felt, only to be told a few days later another way I should be, that was definitely *not* being myself. I finally point blank asked him which he wanted me to do and be. Was I to act in a way that was foreign to me, or be myself? Because I couldn't do both.

He blinked at me in confusion like I'd just put forth some wildly implausible theory about the origins of the universe.

These double-bind expectations rapidly appeared to be the norm. If I was in the office, I should be out in the community more. If I was out in the community, I should be in the office more. No matter what I did, I could never satisfy the demanded expectations since they were constantly shifting.

Then some grossly inappropriate comments started. "I ordered your Madonna mic—you can go bra shopping now." He at least recognized the moment he said it that wasn't appropriate and tried to cover for it by laughing and going, "Don't go reporting me, now." I smiled tightly and tried to laugh it off as well.

Or he'd purposely come into my office for the sole purpose of making fun of someone based on their looks or weight. When I didn't find his disparaging remarks funny, I was being too uptight.

During Christmas Eve rehearsal I requested that I be able to sit down at some point during each of the services as the three bulging discs in my cervical spine would be screaming after eight hours of non-stop standing. He gave me a disgusted look and went, "They didn't tell us you were defective."

While on the surface, none of that seems too awful. Little comments here and there. Trauma triggers. Feeling manhandled. Subtle jabs and comments disguised as jokes. Nothing, when taken individually, really rose to the level of thinking I was in some kind of hostile work environment.

Much of that changed following a Good Friday service, however. We had gone out to grab a drink after the service, along with his wife and another member of the ministry staff. Something political was on the news behind the bar, and whatever happened to be on, it prompted him to lift his beer glass in a toast and say, "God bless Bill Clinton for getting a blow job!"

I was so taken aback by the notion that someone would laud the abuse of power by a President over an intern that I immediately asked for my check and left. Especially someone who wielded that same kind of power over me in many ways.

It was also around this time that I discovered my position was being funded by "gifts and bequests" and there was only one year's worth of funds. I was never informed of this. In fact, I was told there was funding for three years. When I contacted the synod demanding to know why this was not what I'd been presented with, they were equally dumbfounded, saying the three years of funding I'd been presented with was what they'd also been given. The senior was planning on retiring sometime over the next three years, so three years of funding would take us up to that time where I could determine whether this call was working out or not. Three years seemed like a decent amount of time to get the lay of the land.

However, the congregation was told there was funding for only one year, and presented with different financials. During the congregational vote to call me, someone stood and asked, specifically, if I knew there was only one year of funding. It seemed strange to them I'd be willing to move half-way across the country just for a year.

The congregation was told yes, I was aware.

When I confronted the senior pastor after discovering this—because he knew darn well I did not know this—his response was simply, "Yeah, I wondered when you were going to bring that up."

Just that bluntly. Was I supposed to appreciate the honesty *now*?

Whoever had asked that question in the congregational meeting was absolutely correct. I would have never uprooted my life, moved across the country where I had to leave behind my family, friends, and support system, for a call that only had one year of funding. That would have been sheer madness on my part. I'd have held out for something more stable.

That was *also* information that should not have been withheld from me. This was more than just faulty logic and misdirection.

Immediately after I confronted him, he launched into his favorite tactic of nitpicky garbage to deflect away from the fact that he just admitted he lied to both me and the congregation. He pivoted to, "We don't work as a team."

As it was designed to do, I was caught off guard by the sudden shift in conversation that was meant to highlight my perceived deficiencies, directing me away from being the one doing the confronting, to immediately having to go on the defensive. In retrospect, the proper response to that would have been to redirect him back to the issue at hand. Instead, I responded with, "What does that look like for you?"

"Well," he began in an agitated tone of voice. "You left one day at four and I didn't know where you went, and it made me mad because I wound up working until like seven. That really pissed me off." He couldn't tell me what day it was and no, he hadn't bothered asking any of the other staff if I'd told them where I'd gone.

Never mind the fact that he made double my salary and was the actual senior pastor of the congregation. He *should* have been working more.

Then he wanted to know if I felt the entire weight of this congregation rested on my shoulders. That was a trick question, and I knew it—there was no right answer. If I said yes, then I'm making it too much about me. If I said no, then I wasn't working hard enough.

I should have called out the fact that this was a no-win scenario no matter how I answered. Instead, I went with "no" and took the lashing of how he gave "one hundred and ten percent," and I should too.

Suffice it to say it was a lot of manipulative behavior that was designed to keep me off-balance and walking on eggshells. I rapidly discovered he was known for driving away his associates because he made their lives hell.

Despite the fact that I was not hired to run the youth program—we had a youth director for that—he began blaming me for the fact that in just a few short months I had not somehow miraculously turned around the declining numbers in our youth program. When I pointed out that not only was that *not* what I'd been called here to do, as I had made it abundantly clear in my paperwork and interviews that youth ministry was not in my realm of expertise, I stated what I thought was fairly obvious: you don't just turn around a declining program overnight.

He then proceeded to inform me that another associate pastor had apparently done just that: taken a non-existent youth program and had fifty-plus students attending in just a few short months. I doubted the veracity of that claim but had no information one way or another to confirm or deny, so I fell silent. As I so often did.

I began turning to unhealthy coping mechanisms such as eating everything I could find for comfort, and I simply didn't care how I looked anymore. When my mother commented on my weight gain, I told her as much. Food was the only thing that brought me enjoyment. I was not interested in dating, and my life was just one on-going abusive system.

My doctor upped my anxiety and depression medications to their maximum dosage.

I wasn't sure exactly where to turn. In fact, I was not even sure what was happening, to the point that I just knew I was miserable and decided maybe it was simply time for me to get out of ministry. Clearly the problem was me, I was just too broken to do this anymore. I even began sending out resumés and going on interviews for graphic design positions in the area.

I emailed a mentor and friend of mine from seminary, saying I really needed to talk to her about some discernment. I didn't think ministry was my calling anymore, and I began to outline some of the stuff that was going on.

Her response was to call me and say, "Of course we can discuss discernment regarding your calling, but first, we need to talk about how you're being sexually harassed."

Oh.

It can be that way sometimes. So subtle, so subversive, that you don't even identify it as sexual harassment. It wasn't overt and explicit. You simply know it's wrong and something is making you absolutely miserable. The gaslighting, the snide comments, the inappropriate jokes, the blaming, the outbursts of anger: I had normalized all this behavior once before and it nearly killed me, and here it was happening again, being compounded by the fact that my divorce was just barely finalized. The trauma was fresh and real.

What did I do about it, though? There was nothing extreme happening directly to me, just behavior that was whittling away at my soul and my self-esteem day in and day out.

I sought out a therapist to help me cope, only to get told, "Women just have to learn to deal with being sexually harassed. It's simply our reality."

(Note: If a therapist tells you this, do not go back to that therapist.)

What should have been a paradise became another struggle for survival, with the grinning Joker-Cat always looking over my shoulder, reminding me that I still was not safe.

The strings were not yet attached, however, so escape from this twisted illusion of a paradise was still possible and, I assumed, more easily achieved.

You know what happens when you assume.

I believed I could choose not to play. Alice effectively ended her game by kicking the deck of cards down.

I was going to kick the cards down.

I had known two weeks in I was caught in a game and a battle I likely was not going to win. There was already a body count of others who had held my position and the likelihood that I was going to ultimately do anything to change that was slim to none. Systems protect themselves.

Truthfully, I was too tired and exhausted to even try anymore.

So, I called the synod, I informed them it wasn't working out, outlined the reasons why, and said I wanted to begin the mobility process, even though I was only a few months in.

I kicked the cards, and immediately discovered: escape from Wonderland is never that simple. Just deciding not to play the game was apparently not an option.

The response I received was, "Are you being overly sensitive due to your marriage?"

I had divorced a narcissist. I was no stranger to what if felt like to be gaslit. That question sounded very much to my ears like, "Are you sure you experienced what you think you experienced?"

My hackles rose, my walls went up. I immediately realized I could not turn to the people who I'd always been told were there to help me because I believed, at that moment, they were not actually there to help me.

Still, I reflected on the question, then proceeded to point out that in addition to that information they'd just "forgotten" to tell me, they had also neglected to tell me there had been eighteen congregation members who sent letters to the synod about three months prior to my arrival, saying the senior pastor was unfit to continue being a pastor and needed to retire. They all left the congregation in a mass exodus before I started.

I found that out when other congregation members brought it to my attention, and I added it to the list of things I had not been told when I asked about red flags before accepting the call.

By this time, I had also become privy to many of the rumors that were circulating around town regarding this church's reputation, most of which

I ignored because I don't indulge rumors. Still, given my own experiences, when a phlebotomist at the doctor's office asked me where I worked and I told her, it caught my attention when she said, "Oh, yeah. I used to go to that church. It's the sex church."

I blinked and asked what she meant by that.

She meant what I thought she meant.

Still. These were not things I witnessed myself. They were all rumors and hearsay.

That was until the youth director came to me with concerns about inappropriate comments the senior pastor had made to her regarding some confirmation students.

That wasn't a rumor I could just ignore. One of my staff had just informed me of inappropriate behavior and comments regarding minors and to ignore that would have been gross negligence on my part. I had no choice.

First, I went to a couple of council members with the youth director so she could tell exactly what happened as a first-hand witness. They agreed it was terrible but seemed at a loss as to what to do about that. I then made my required report to the synod, gave them the youth director's information, and left it in their hands to deal with accordingly. The youth director wound up quitting shortly thereafter.

That senior pastor did eventually retire. When that happened, I received a call and was warned that if I talked about my experiences, they likely would not be able to place me in another call.

I felt I was being silenced. I think *they* thought they were protecting me.

The problem is, when you're unable to speak your truth—it's suffocating.

Everything I thought I knew in the realm of love and trust turned out to be incorrect. Love did not equal a happy or healthy marriage when the love itself was a lie. The Church, which I'd always believed to be a source of integrity and founded on doing "the right thing" turned out to be, like so many other things in the world, simply a power structure that attempted to protect itself by any means necessary. These were hard realities to discover and come to terms with.

It was a shock to my system, because my experience back in my previous call had been positive in terms of having an entire faith community caring for me. They were what kept me going; they were what gave me life. I'd have collapsed without them. They showed grace and support during one of the most trying times in my life.

To be treated in such a dramatically different way by a system that absolutely knew the situation I had just left behind felt like a deep and utter betrayal. Not to mention, I had not developed any relationships or friendships where I was, so I felt totally and utterly alone.

A short time later, I received a phone call from another pastor. They proceeded to tell me about how that pastor had been inappropriate with them.

As I listened to them tell their story, I froze. I was dumbfounded. I didn't know this pastor well, I'd maybe been introduced to them at a synod event one time, so the fact that they were calling me and telling me their story stunned me.

I also remembered that I was told not to talk about my situation. Were they a plant? Were they sent by the synod to try and see if I was going to talk about it?

So I said absolutely nothing in response. Just silence.

Years later I would discover more details surrounding that critical information I'd not been informed of until I'd already signed the dotted line. Needless to say, things were actually *not* just fine. But in their infinite wisdom, the synod still decided to place a female abuse survivor into this context.

That particular synod staff is now all retired as well, but I remain. Still wary, still scarred, still unable to fully trust. It wears on you not being able to tell your truths. Confidentiality continues to keep me veiled in a certain amount of silence, still fearful of the repercussions of disclosing too much. Yet, in order to tell my story, I had to tell at least part of what happened directly to me. Other people's stories are their stories. They're not for me to divulge.

Whether it was my marriage or my job, I was thrust into someone else's game where I was not given the rules and was desperately trying to figure out how to play the game without all the information. It's a disorienting place to be and live.

Alice in Wonderland, like the story of Adam and Eve, is also a story about a loss of innocence and transitioning from childhood into adulthood. In so many ways, I also had to "grow up" in terms of learning and experiencing some realities in life that had never been part of my world.

Despite a career in Hollywood prior to this, I was naive to the ways of true manipulation and abuse. In Hollywood, the abuse was fairly clear. It wasn't hidden. It was known. It was talked about. It was right there for everyone to see and recognize.

I mean, I worked for Disney, which owned Miramax productions. Miramax was still run by Harvey Weinstein at that time. While I did not directly witness or experience the kind of sexual harassment and assault as other women, let's just say Weinstein-like behavior was not an uncommon practice in Hollywood. Nor was it relegated to only heterosexual men in power. One of my own supervisors in animation was also later accused of sexual harassment and misconduct. The allegations did not surprise me in the least when they came out.

But that's Hollywood. No one has illusions that Hollywood is an ethical or moral place to live and work.

Marriage and the church, however, I believe I still viewed through a certain child-like lens, believing in the best of both. That neither would intentionally attempt to hurt me, much less kill me.

Yet, both nearly did.

While not my denomination, the recent allegations that have come to light in lieu of the investigation of misconduct by pastors in the Southern Baptist Convention and the sweeping cover-ups that occurred by those in authority speaks to the depth and reality of these problems. Especially their most recent move to disfellowship churches that have women pastors on staff. They manage to keep a database of predators with over seven hundred sexual abuse complaints that they claim they "simply can't do anything about," but have a hit list of churches with women in leadership positions that they're quick to remove within months. Because females preaching are more dangerous than sexual predators, apparently.

I'd like to say such problems are relegated to denominations that don't value the voices and roles of women in the church. Reality is, my own denomination has a body count that is embarrassingly large. My own situation was not an outlier.

Whether it's Hollywood, politics or the Church, these scandals are typically more commonplace than they would like to let on. The systems have learned how to protect themselves, how to consolidate their power, and how to keep victims shrouded in silence.

Some of us get caught in this shroud of silence, unable to speak openly about the truth of our experiences. Admittedly it is not simply because of the fear of losing one's job that keeps us silent, but also the realization that many people will be devastated if they discover people they love and care about were involved. It makes our ability to do our job impossible should the truth come out at that point.

For me, I at least was able to have my experience validated. Other people told their stories and their experiences. I had the opportunity to forge a new path out of Wonderland. While still caught in some ways in the game, it's a game I better understand now. It's a game where I know how the rules will change, who to trust, and who not to trust.

Alice faced down all the threats in front of her. She knocked over the deck of cards that were sent to attack her and they turned into nothing more than leaves falling on her face as she awakened from her dream.

While I do wish that much of what I went through had indeed only been a dream—or rather a nightmare—it was all too real for myself and others.

Seventeen

Bound

*"Stab the body and it heals,
but injure the heart and the wound lasts a lifetime."*

— Mineko Iwasaki

When the Evil Queen demands the Huntsman bring her Snow White's heart, we don't really think: "Why the heart?" I mean, let's face it, the Huntsman was able to easily exchange it out for the heart of a pig instead and fool the Queen. So clearly, the demand for the heart was not exactly a fool-proof identifying feature. So why the heart? What symbolic power does the heart hold that the Queen would have wanted it?

Following my first year of seminary, I did a summer Clinical Pastoral Education (CPE) unit at Bergen-Mercy Hospital in Omaha, Nebraska. This is a requirement that seminary students in my denomination (Evangelical Lutheran Church in America, or ELCA) are required to do where essentially we act as hospital chaplains. It's a difficult summer unit because you spend a lot of time having to be self-reflective, analyzing your own responses, emotions, and personality. I frequently felt like our group sessions where we would discuss our patient interactions with other students and our supervisor were more of a group therapy session than anything else.

I was assigned to the cardiac unit, providing pastoral care to people who were having any variety of heart procedures done. Not that there is really any major surgery that doesn't induce anxiety, but I think heart and brain surgery are probably right up there in terms of understanding that if something goes wrong, you don't live without a heart or a brain.

During this time, I really began thinking about the importance of "the heart," not just in terms of how our bodies need the heart to pump blood and deliver the necessary oxygen to our brains and perform other functions, but its importance in our emotional well-being.

In Jewish thought, the heart is more than just a mere organ that pumps blood and keeps you alive. It is the seat of the emotional and intellectual life of a human being. "Keep your heart with all diligence; for out of it are the issues of life" (Prov. 4:23), refers to the moral and spiritual as well as the physical life. Many of the things we now prescribe as "mental" thought (knowing, feeling, and willing) were considered matters of the heart to the Biblical writers.

Many cultures assumed that the heart was the seat of intelligence, and without an advanced understanding of physiology, it makes sense. The heart is the only moving organ in the body, and strong emotions cause the heartbeat to race. When the heart stops beating, a person is dead. The heart was the metaphor of the mind and all mental and emotional activity.

The heart is where we make choices. So the concept of the "heart" is best understood as the "inner person"—the seat of our mind (thoughts), emotions (feelings), and will (intentions).

As the seat of emotion, it contains all modes of feeling: from the lowest physical forms, such as hunger and thirst, to the highest spiritual forms of reverence and remorse. There is a Jewish midrash that lists over sixty emotions of the heart.[1] Among these emotions: "the heart sees, hears, speaks, falls, stands, rejoices, weeps, comforts, sorrows."

As the seat of intention, it is self-directing and self-determining. It is in the heart that the heart becomes conscious of itself and of its own operations. It recognizes its own suffering. It is the seat of self-consciousness.

As the whole physical and psychical life is centralized in the heart, so the whole moral life springs from and issues out of it.

This idea is no longer outside the bounds of scientific research, either. The new field of neurocardiology has increasingly shown that our hearts actually do have a much larger role than simply pumping our lifeblood.

One of the early pioneers in neurocardiology, Dr. J. Andrew Armour, introduced the concept of a functional "heart brain" in 1991. His work revealed that the heart has a complex intrinsic nervous system that is sufficiently sophisticated to qualify as a "little brain" in its own right. The heart's brain is an intricate network of several types of neurons, neurotransmitters, proteins and support cells like those found in the brain proper. Its elaborate circuitry enables it to act independently of the cranial brain—to learn, remember, and even feel and sense.[2]

The human heart, they have discovered, contains a complex network of neurons that make up an intrinsic nervous system. These neurons transmit

---

1. Kadden, Barbara Binder, "An Understanding of the Heart—Biddah Binat HaLev," reformjudaism.org, 2023.

2. Armour, J. Andrew, "The Brain in the Heart," Neurocardiology, Heartmath Institute, 2015.

the heart's signals to the brain, and the two organs actually work together. Neural pathways have been discovered that allow the heart to either inhibit or stimulate the brain's electrical activity—to actually overrule the mind.

I wish I could say I have figured out how to "tame my heart," to allow my brain to overrule my heart rather than the other way around. Unfortunately, we seem wired to experience, crave, and desire incredible love and affection. There's no greater feeling than the euphoria of new love that you feel for someone.

And all too often, I continue to allow my heart to overrule my brain. As the saying goes, "the heart wants what the heart wants."

But for every action, there's an equal and opposite reaction, and when it comes to the ecstasy of true love, that reaction is a gut-wrenching pain, a deep void of sadness, and feelings of seemingly eternal loneliness. When you are grieving and feeling that intense emotional pain, you can physically feel it in your chest and heart. This isn't a trick of the mind. Your heart feels these things and transmits those feelings to your brain.

A friend of mine recently asked the question, "Is there any pain worse than a broken heart?" Emotional pain for me feels, in many ways, worse even than physical pain.

I can dull physical pain. I can take medication to alleviate physical pain. Emotional pain? That just has to run its course. I have found going on short-term anti-depressants can help, but I'm certainly not a doctor. I was raised by one enough to know that about myself. So I cannot speak to or recommend that for others.

What I do know is I've been through a lot of heartache in my life. I've had three major loves in my life. The ending of each of those relationships was devastating. They hurt in ways that are difficult even to describe despite my best attempts.

Obviously, my marriage was the most traumatic and was only the second time I had made the choice to walk away from someone, rather than the other way around. It was the first time I had to leave someone I loved because I was worried about my survival.

When the Bible talks about two people becoming one flesh, I understand what it means. It's literally like having a limb ripped off, your heart physically torn in two.

When I was lying on the floor sobbing, struggling to breathe, it was like you could literally feel the tearing of the heart, its contents leaking out into the rest of my body like a poison.

It's not tough to see that reality depicted in this painting.

When your life's plans are thrown aside, and your life lies in ruins at the bottom of the deep dark pit you have fallen into, realizing that you are, in fact, not the director of your life's drama, your heart breaks. It strips you of everything as you are surrounded by that dark despair to the point that you eventually hold out the pieces of that heart to God and say, "Here—do what you want with this. It's broken—and I can't fix it."

Yet we try to fix it anyway. Hearts are fragile things, and when they've been trampled, abused, and ripped apart, we find ways to try to protect them from that ever happening again.

So we build fences. We chain and padlock that which we once freely gave to others, but now carefully guard. We find ourselves prisoners of our own hearts because we're afraid of what it might mean to let someone in again and make ourselves vulnerable. We isolate our heart and place it many times in the middle of a barren wasteland and desert—which isn't all bad when you're letting the ickiness and ooze of a past hurt drain out of it.

Such a process is not always destructive—but is in its own way a type of healing. The "yuck" needs to spill out in order for healing and wholeness to begin. It's better to let it do that in a barren wasteland than somewhere that the ooze might harm the surrounding landscape.

Taking time alone to heal is healthy, actually.

That's not all this painting conveys, however.

While on the one hand, this painting depicts the necessity to protect the heart, to try and mitigate the damage that's been done to it by not letting anyone or anything in again, the reality also is that life at times is a storm that's breaking everything apart, and you're just trying to hold it together.

The chains can clearly serve two purposes: to both protect and keep others out, while also holding together the remnants. One is only able to hold the pieces together many times by building protective barriers. We all have our coping and survival mechanisms, after all.

Some people leave these chains in place for the rest of their lives. Others, like me, allow chinks to start whittling away at the links that surround them.

For the first five years after my divorce, while I was in "survival mode" simply trying to navigate my way through both my personal and work trauma, dating was honestly the last thing I wanted or cared about. I didn't care that I'd gained weight—I had no interest in trying to attract anyone anyway and food was one of the few things that could give me comfort.

As the years passed and I no longer found myself in an abusive situation, I began to emerge from my haze. I began to try to and see my life as not being just jumping from one battle to another. I decided I needed to start living life again, not just surviving.

I lost sixty pounds. I began swimming and getting in shape.

Now you'd think that after my disastrous marriage, I would have opted to never touch another dating site again in my life, right?

While I had my heart bound up in chains, it hadn't been hard to not date, because there was literally no one I had met in the past five years that even piqued my interest enough to think about dating. I'd joined in-person meet-up groups where I lived just to try and make friends outside the church. There were simply no prospects.

So when I did feel like trying to date again, I had to go the route of dating apps. Online dating had changed in just those few short years. Now everything was an "app," and you would just look at a picture. If they bothered to fill out a short bio or description, bonus. Most did not, or if they did, it didn't really say much.

Still, in December of 2019 I began talking with a guy who lived about forty minutes away. We Facetimed and chatted a lot before finally deciding to meet in January. He was about ten years younger than I was, which freaked me out a little as I'd never dated anyone younger than me by more than a year or two, but when you get to be in your late forties, it's not like there's a huge difference between that and your late thirties.

We met just a few days before my forty-eighth birthday. It's not lost on me that I had met my ex-husband just a few days after my thirty-eighth birthday. Or that I'd been dumped *on* my twenty-eighth birthday.

The date went well. We had a lovely dinner along the river and then sat on the beach under the moonlight and just talked for a few hours. I had high hopes this would turn into something more.

We got together again a week or so later, and then something strange happened.

We were supposed to have dinner one Monday evening and watch the national championship game together. He was a huge Ohio State fan, and they were playing, but I'd decided not to hold that against him. He'd gone back to school to become a teacher and was at the library studying for one of his classes. It got later and later, and finally I determined we would not be going to dinner. I knew his school work was important and had to come first, so I just shrugged it off and said we could still watch the game together. He hemmed and hawed and said he didn't feel he should be out late on a school night, because, of all things, his seventy-year-old roommate would think he wasn't taking his classes seriously.

Now I should probably back up a little and divulge that he was a recovering alcoholic and his roommate was also his AA sponsor. You guessed it. I didn't hold these things against him because addictions are rough, and I had no issues supporting not drinking alcohol. I only very rarely consumed myself these days, so I naively saw this as a non-issue. (Yes, my whole not holding things against people is my absolute and utter downfall every single time, so you can guess where this relationship is headed already.)

Still, this seemed really strange, and I let him know that I was not impressed by this reasoning. At that point, things kind of went downhill, and we didn't go out again before I left for a Holy Land trip at the end of the month.

Then Covid happened. On the day we were returning back from Tel-Aviv, we began receiving alerts that flights from China were being cancelled. By the time I got back, it was only a few short weeks before we all were given orders to stay home as the nation went into lock-down mode.

Sitting around home with nothing to do while everyone is in a state of anxiety apparently causes some of us to reach out and make contact with those we really shouldn't.

It was Easter when I heard from him again. We'd done a service at the church with just the praise team that we livestreamed to our congregation. We would not re-open our doors for several more months.

At that time, he apologized, said he'd just kind of been going through something and trying to figure out what he wanted back in January. I said okay and, being me...well, you guessed it... I forgave him. (Cue the eyeroll.)

Everything was shut down so beyond doing some Facetime stuff, we didn't have the opportunity to actually go on any dates. We finally decided we could meet up for outdoor activities. We went snorkeling, he tried to teach me how to surf, and we went kayaking.

Still, there was something that didn't quite seem right. We always got together during the day, never in the evening. He claimed he had AA meetings every night, but I began to notice that when we would Facetime, he never wanted his seventy-year-old roommate to know we were talking, to the point he'd even sometimes just hang up on me when the other man would walk into the room.

One day I finally stated that I felt like "the other woman." He was confused, and I explained that I felt like he was using me to cheat on someone else. I finally asked: "Are you in a relationship with your roommate?"

He paused.

My stomach lurched at that pause which could mean only one thing.

"Well, not right now, no," he finally confessed.

That was the end of that.

I had zero interest in those games, nor was I interested in whatever strange manipulation was going on with the seventy-year-old male roommate, who also happened to be his AA sponsor. The power dynamic aside of a sponsor living with his sponsee, the younger man was completely dependent on the older for having a place to live. When he was forced to confess his relationship with the older man, he cried, "I can't tell him I'm not gay! I don't want to live on the street!" There was a mess of control and manipulation I wanted no part of. Not to mention I learned the hard way that just because an addict isn't drinking, doesn't mean they're sober. They're still engaging in the same habits of lying and sneaking around, whether alcohol is involved or not.

This was my first attempt at dating post-divorce, so you see how well that went.

Actually, I take that back. I went out on one date with a local therapist I'd led a support group with for abuse victims. When the group dissolved, he asked me out to a lunch date, which took me by surprise. Last I knew he was engaged.

That had been called off. So, we went to lunch. Where he attempted to persuade me to sleep with him and when I turned him down, he informed me I didn't know what I was missing. He then blocked me on Facebook and I never heard from him again. Which, honestly, was just fine with me.

My second legitimate attempt at dating was far more complicated and was much more devastating for a lot of reasons.

My story with that guy from Aviation Challenge who I went to visit in Florida when I was twenty-three, only to find out he still had his seventeen-year-old chippy of a girlfriend, wasn't completely over.

Back in 2010, prior to my meeting my future ex-husband, we reconnected via Facebook. There were apologies made; he was married now and still lived in Florida while I was back in Nebraska. What had happened between us had been nearly fifteen years earlier. I'd missed having him as a friend. There still was this inexplicable tie I felt to him, so I allowed him back into my life, albeit only virtually. The occasional email or Facebook "hello," but nothing much beyond that.

A few months after I got engaged, I received an email from him: he was getting divorced.

I would be lying if at that moment I hadn't felt a twinge of regret at the timing. But I loved my fiancé and at that juncture had no idea what was to come. I was also a realist. He lived in Florida. I lived in Nebraska. We hadn't even spoken in person for over fifteen years, and I had to set aside ridiculous romantic fairy tale fantasies that played in my head.

Plus, we'd played that game once before, and it had ended terribly. I carefully filed whatever lingering emotional connection I had to him away under, "not possible," and promptly moved on. To the point I even forgot to mention to him that I was getting married. He found out when I replied to an email several months after my marriage and I had a different last name.

Oops. Sorry about that.

When things in my own marriage began falling apart, he had randomly emailed me asking me how life was going, and I responded by spilling my guts on everything that was happening with the arrests, the courts, the mortgage, the daughter. I'd given him my number some time ago when he was going through his own divorce in case he just needed a friendly voice to talk to, though we hadn't actually spoken on the phone since 1996.

He called me that evening, concerned about everything going on in my life. It was weird to hear his voice after all that time. Still, I was married and despite all the problems I was having, this was nothing more than a friendship.

Yet somehow we easily fell back into our old banter and talked for a few hours.

Eventually, when I did file for divorce, we continued to remain friends, and both commiserated over the heartache and pain that was involved in getting divorced.

When I eventually moved to Florida, I realized I would only be living an hour away from him. This was not by design or desire. In fact, I only wound up interviewing in Florida because when a friend of mine found out I was looking for a new call, she reached out asking if I had any interest in Florida. Sun? Beach? No more shoveling snow? Sure, why not? The close proximity in where we lived didn't really translate into much anyway, as being a pilot, he was constantly gone, and so we tended to only get together once every six months if we were lucky.

This was our pattern for about six years. We'd hang out, watch some football, go to dinner, maybe head up to the Kennedy Space Center for the day—do the things we'd always enjoyed and had connected with each other over when we were seventeen.

Now at some point during our friendship, he'd made the joke that when we turned fifty, if we were both still single, maybe we would get together. The whole Monica and Chandler deal from *Friends*. I forced myself to brush this comment off because I knew he didn't mean it. That doesn't mean it wasn't something I secretly wanted, however.

During one of his visits, we were at dinner at a local Cajun restaurant and I jokingly stated, "You know, I turn forty-nine in less than six months. That means in less than eighteen months, I'm going to be fifty, and if you don't help me find someone, you're going to be stuck with me."

He laughed and said, "You were mad when I first suggested that, but that doesn't sound so bad now, does it?"

I refrained from saying it had never sounded bad, but I wasn't about to let him know that.

We finished dinner, and as we were heading out of the restaurant, he reached over and grabbed my hand as we walked down the sidewalk. Stunned, I wasn't even sure what he was trying to do. I stared at him, pulled my hand away, going, "What...what are you doing?"

"Well, I was trying to hold your hand..." he said in an exasperated tone of voice.

Still feeling a bit stunned, I relinquished my hand and let him hold it as we then walked along the riverfront just talking for a while. The evening didn't end with simple handholding.

Were we living a real life *When Harry Met Sally* type of scenario? Two friends after years and years finally romantically get together and live happily after because, as he had stated so many years earlier, we really *were* soulmates after all?

Spoiler alert: No.

After spending a few days hanging a ceiling fan and determining a few other projects he would do around my house the next time he came to visit (wait, he was actually making plans to come see me again? He never did that!), he went back home and we didn't really talk again until the next month when

I went down to help him install *his* ceiling fans. We had a good laugh when he was ready to take them back because they didn't work and I simply pointed out to him that he hadn't unwrapped the batteries from the plastic they were in and that would probably solve the problem of the remotes not working. There were many swear words at that juncture after he tried my suggestion and they magically began working.

My having saved him the trouble of tearing down and returning perfectly good ceiling fans aside, he decided to clarify our previous visit, that he was not interested in a relationship. He was done with relationships and didn't want that.

My heart sank a little bit, but okay. I accepted that and went back home. I figured that was the end of that, I'd probably see him in another six months or year, per our usual pattern. And we'd go back to being "just friends" or something. Just forget about the handholding and the other romantic overtures.

Then in early November he wanted to come visit and see me again. A few weeks later, he was going to be terminating one of his flights near where I lived. Did I want to catch a ride on his jet and he'd bring me back the next day? Then he was up visiting again right before Christmas and helped me decorate my house.

Needless to say, I was confused as to what was going on. So I finally asked, and again got the answer, "No, I don't want a relationship."

Things kind of continued like this through May when I finally had to push the issue and wanted to know what we were doing exactly. That's when he informed me he had absolutely no romantic interest in me whatsoever, that he was never going to love me the way I wanted to be loved, he couldn't help comparing me to his ex-wife, and he just didn't have those same kind of feelings for me.

But you know, let's still be friends.

I'm not sure on what planet guys think this is a thing.

If you want to stab a woman in the heart, telling her she doesn't live up to the standard of the ex-wife who was a train wreck that cheated on you constantly, that's a pretty effective way to do it. I told him I really didn't want to try and remain friends because it was just too hard to be around him. I would always want what I couldn't have.

Despite all the "I don't want to be in a relationship" protestations from him, I couldn't help it. I'd let my long-buried feelings and desires for him resurface. I'd allowed myself to have some kind of ridiculous hope that he'd eventually change his mind.

I'd let the chains around my heart loosen and I'd let him in...again.

Because the heart overrides the brain sometimes.

Because I still, after everything, wanted the fairy tale. The Disney-type, not the Brothers' Grimm type that always ends horribly. Not the type I was becoming far too familiar with.

It didn't help that so many of my friends were convinced—this was the guy for me. Friends who had met him were all like, "Of course he loves you, he's just scared." You know how those conversations go. Even a friend who is a "psychic" for a living stated, "Girl, he absolutely has all the feels for you. I can see it."

So much for "psychics." Living proof they are absolute bunk.

Again, I only had one friend, my best friend who had seen me through the crying puddles on the floor during my divorce, had the gumption to say, "I don't like how he treats you."

One of these days, I'll take my own advice of listening to my friends when they tell me things like this. This wasn't one of those days, unfortunately.

Thirty-two years after we had first met, my *When Harry Met Sally* hopes and dreams crashed and burned after we went to see *Maverick,* a movie *he'd* wanted to see together because *Top Gun* had been kind of the theme of the Aviation Challenge where we had originally met.

There's a part of me that says I should have known better. People don't really ever change and I should have known that.

I knew how much I'd changed over the years and I had truly thought he had as well, that he'd matured, that he'd never have gone down this road unless he was serious about it. That having his heart ripped out when his wife cheated on him and left him had taught him a few things about life and love. That you don't mess with another person's heart and emotions.

It really sucks being that wrong so much of the time.

Here I had finally let the chains around my heart unwind just a little with someone I had spent years cultivating a friendship with that I thought I could trust with that heart—only to have it trampled once again.

In a lot of ways, the ending of that relationship was almost harder than the ending of my marriage, for different reasons. There was a much longer history. I'd gone through so much with him being that person who sat and listened and commiserated with me during my vulnerable years of divorce.

It was a different kind of betrayal, but a betrayal, nonetheless. I still could not figure out why. Why had he gone through the trouble of altering our friendship? Why had he taken my hand that evening and made romantic overtures? Why for a few months had he paid so much more attention to me than he had in years past, while still claiming he didn't want a relationship?

Those aren't questions I'll have an answer to. Once again, I got to feel the pain of everything in my heart oozing out. It still brings me to tears to talk about and write about it. Thirty-two years is a long time to be connected to someone just to have it all go up in smoke like that. The loss of yet another dream and hope.

A part of me wonders if I'd kept those chains in place, would we still be friends and I would not have had to feel that pain again?

Once again, I don't know why love is such an elusive thing for me. Other people seem to fall in love at the drop of a hat. I go in ten year intervals—never with a happy ending. So I can only assume at fifty-eight, I will once again begin this process all over again with someone new.

The question will be what state will those chains around my heart be in? Will they tighten around my heart even more, keeping everything and everyone out?

Admittedly, that's not really in my nature, and sometimes that makes me angry. I want to be content with my life the way it is. I want to stop desiring companionship. God has made it pretty clear that no romantic relationship for me is going to go well.

So why do I keep doing this to myself? Why do I let the chains loosen? The walls down?

It's like the moment I let the chains down to let someone in, my heart falls apart and spills all over the place as it gets trampled and hurt once again.

One of my biggest problems is not that I don't trust others, it's that I no longer trust myself to make good decisions. Clearly I make disastrously poor choices when it comes to matters of the heart. No, I can't trust others. But I can trust myself even less.

Still, I keep clinging to hope.

I keep hoping one of these times, my fairy tale will not be of the tragic, sad variety, but of the happily ever after kind.

Eighteen

Release

> *"Letting go doesn't mean that you don't care about someone anymore. It's just realizing that the only person you really have control over is yourself."*
>
> — Deborah Reber

MOST FAIRY TALES DO not venture into the realm of forgiveness. Some versions of *Cinderella* attempt to go this route where she forgives the stepsisters of their cruelty, but more often than not, the evil characters get what's coming to them. Rarely at the hands of the victim, however.

I've often wondered why themes of forgiveness are so rare in fairy tales, and yet so prominent in the Bible. The short nature of the fairy tale medium is perhaps one reason. Forgiveness is complicated. Much more complicated than most fairy tales have time for, plus they usually are trying to send a message about evil people getting their come-uppance. It's a moral tale, after all. Not reality.

Because the reality is, forgiving someone who has harmed you is hard. Renewing a relationship with someone who has harmed you can be even harder—and it is not always safe to renew a relationship with someone who is toxic and destructive. It's much easier to hope for people who have done terrible things to dance on hot coals or be boiled in vats of boiling water or having their eyes pecked out by birds. (All of which are variant endings to some of our favorite well-known fairy tales.)

While I'd been able to renew my friendship with pilot dude following his apologies because of my capacity for forgiveness, I knew I would never get an apology from my ex-husband for the hell he put me through. In fact, in his mind, I'm the one who undoubtedly put him through hell. Years later he was still blaming me for much of his situation, accusing his brother and me of conspiring to steal all of his money, of which there had been none. One does not always need an apology to choose to forgive or to choose to renew a relationship, however.

I was certain that renewing any sort of relationship with my ex-husband would not be a safe venture. He had not changed based on the information I was receiving from other individuals. I don't believe God wanted me placing myself into those crosshairs again to try and attempt to change someone only God can change.

What I could do, however, was release the relationship.

ONCE UPON A NIGHTMARE

The late Archbishop, Desmond Tutu, in his book, *The Book of Forgiving*, discusses the "Four-fold Path of Forgiving," which consists of:

1. Telling the story
2. Naming the hurt
3. Granting forgiveness
4. Renewing or releasing the relationship

Over the years, my art and my writing have been steps one and two—telling my story and naming the hurt. I've used these pages to tell my story. I've named the hurt of what happened. It's the realization that the one thing I wanted most in this world was used against me to manipulate me so I could be a shield of sorts for all his legal problems. That level of betrayal and hurt runs deep. Recognizing that all your hopes and dreams for a future were torn and shattered amidst a web of lies and deceit is beyond devastating. That the one thing you wanted most in this world—to simply be loved—was all a lie.

It does a number on you when your self-esteem might not be the best anyway, when you've struggled your entire life to find real connection with another person, struggled to feel loved and cared for in a certain way, only to realize that the person who claimed to be that one person—was lying and only using you.

I waited thirty-eight years to get married. You'd have thought by waiting that long, you'd get it a little closer to right.

And then they systematically tried to destroy your life by going after your friends, your family, your career, your reputation, and your finances.

Forgiving that is a tall order.

To be fair, my anger at him is what gave me strength during my divorce. It's what kept me from caving, from being able to be manipulated into letting him back into my life.

I had to be angry. It was necessary to stay alive. I needed my anger.

Once the divorce was finally over, however, he seemed to know that I was no longer a toy that he could play with anymore, and he left me alone. I was able to breathe a sigh of relief for a time.

Until I discovered he'd moved close to where I lived a year later. Admittedly, it initially terrified me to know he was only three hours away again.

Yet I knew I couldn't let him consume my life any more than he already had. I did what I could to not let him occupy my mental and emotional space.

I was lucky that I had been able to go "no contact." So many women are tied to their narcissists through children. I was able to break free and try to start my life over, such that it was.

Once the chaos died down, and the threat seemed to abate, I began to wonder what forgiveness might actually look like for me.

I'd also like to point out that one of the worst things you can do to an abuse victim is to try to force them or shame them into forgiving before they're ready. Telling them things like, "You don't really have Jesus in your heart," if they don't just forgive someone for the harm they've done is spiritually abusive. People have to come to it in their own time. And when a situation is ongoing, it is not appropriate to expect them to forgive ongoing abuse.

While the abuse had seemingly stopped due to having gone no contact, renewing the relationship was clearly not going to be an option. Releasing it on the other hand—was that something I was capable of doing? How would I even go about that? I still had anxiety triggers, so how could I release something I had no control over?

Tutu described the process of releasing a relationship as how you free yourself from victimhood and trauma. "You can choose not to have someone in your life any longer, but you have released the relationship only when you have truly chosen the path without wishing that person ill. Releasing is refusing to let an experience or a person occupy space in your head or heart any longer. It is releasing not only the relationship but your old story of the relationship."

I was able to not wish him ill. Truly I had never wanted anything bad for him. I only wanted him to leave me alone, and I didn't want him hurting anyone else either.

Sadly, I did not have control over that last part. It wasn't long after he moved near me that I eventually heard from a woman whom he had been renting a room from. She'd been an acquaintance of his during the time we were married, and I'd cut her out of my life like so many of his friends once I filed for divorce. My ex tended to use the people around him to harass me, and quite frankly, I didn't need to explain myself to any of them. So I simply cut them loose.

Still, she reached out, stating, "You know, I was just thinking about you. 'He's not who you think he is' is something you said to me, and now I realize what you meant."

Like everyone in his orbit, once you served a purpose, once you were no longer of benefit to him, he turned on you. It didn't help matters that she did not see him in a romantic light, and he took that personally, as narcissists do. So he set about trying to destroy her life as well. He had gone to her school claiming he had taken her tests and sat in on classes for her, and that she had plagiarized her work. This prompted the school to launch an investigation. She came looking for help to fight what he was trying to do to her.

I obliged as much as I could. Though the last thing I wanted was for him to turn his sights on me ever again.

Soon, she was telling me of another woman who had come to her looking for help because he was threatening her as well.

I drew the line at this point. I simply couldn't get involved.

Whatever her issues she would have to fight him with whatever he was doing to her. I wasn't interested in revenge. I certainly wasn't interested in him coming after me again. I just wished he would leave people alone.

Believe it or not, I prayed for God to change him. For there to be something that eventually got through to him. I knew this was not likely, but I prayed for it anyway. Miracles did happen.

I also was very keenly aware of Jesus' command to forgive seventy times seven.

It's one thing to forgive an accident or a mistake. It's another to try and forgive a serial abuser, someone who doesn't care what kind of pain and chaos they cause other people. In fact, forgiving and not holding someone accountable in such a case can be more problematic and destructive, and that's simply not what God desires for us and our relationships.

I think of the Jesus and Thomas story. Yes, I know most like to call this the "doubting Thomas" story, but I see that story differently. Thomas isn't demanding to see anything the rest of the disciples haven't already experienced. But Thomas is very specific about what he wants and needs to see: The wounds in Jesus' hands and side.

I'm not certain what Thomas' thinking here is, but what strikes me is that Thomas is willing to face not only a resurrected Jesus—but a Jesus that still bears the marks of his torture and death.

A Jesus who does not erase the signs of the sin that was done against him.

I think Jesus' appearance with these wounds, and his invitation to Thomas to touch those wounds, is tied to Jesus' earlier statement to the other disciples about retaining and forgiving sins.

No Jesus is not giving permission to not forgive or to hold a grudge when he says if you retain a sin, it is retained—he's giving a warning about what happens if you do not confront and deal with the sin that has happened.

If you don't confront it and you instead retain it—it festers and becomes destructive.

If you gloss over it or minimize it, you are retaining it, and it does no one any good. If you tried to hide the truth of the harm that was done—that retains it because it can't be dealt with in the light of day. In fact, it causes you to become an enabler of abuse, which neither loves the person who has been harmed, nor does it love the person who is doing the harmful act.

Jesus clearly has forgiven his disciples for their betrayal, denial, and desertion.

Jesus knows that forgiveness is the only way forward.

That the only way for there to be a future between humanity and the divine is for forgiveness to be manifested.

But forgiveness does not mean denying or pretending like the injury never happened. Forgiveness does not mean there is no justice or no accountability. Even if you choose to renew the relationship, it has forever changed—which means things will never be as they were before.

And in some cases, like mine, renewing the relationship was simply not safe. It would not be life-giving. It would only perpetuate more abuse.

Forgiveness at this point becomes more about me than about him. I had to release my anger, my hatred, or whatever it was that was holding me captive, so that I could have a future that was free from holding onto anger and animosity, but that does not mean that there is necessarily a future with that person going forward.

So while that person may retain their sin—once it's brought it into the light and told the truth about it—it can be released.

Releasing that person is still a process. You can't heal a broken bone if you don't first acknowledge it's broken and then set it—and that can be painful, but it's necessary to properly heal.

If you don't, it doesn't heal right and will likely just break again.

I realized I must face the wounds, face the scars. Stick my hands in them and feel how real those hurts are. Let others see the pain and the hurt and know about it.

Forgiveness does not say that what was done was permissible or all right. Forgiveness is instead an invitation to find healing and peace.

It opens the space for peace between two people.

The victim cannot have peace without forgiving.

The perpetrator cannot have peace without being forgiven.

The invitation to forgive is an invitation to search out the perpetrator's humanity.

Which when you're dealing with a narcissist, sociopath, psychopath, or any of the other myriad of personality disorders, finding the humanity in the other can be extremely difficult. Many of my friends referred to my ex as a monster on many occasions.

Again, Desmond Tutu reminds us of the problems with dehumanizing someone. Indeed, what he did was monstrous, but if we call him a monster, that actually lets him off the hook to some degree.

Tutu writes, "To relegate someone to the level of monster is to deny that person's ability to change and ability to take away that person's accountability for his or her actions and behavior."

That statement has stuck with me over the years. It made me think of the story of Adam and Eve and that underlying question: are we more like God, or more like the animals we were created alongside? This is truly the dilemma we face as humans. Humanity is supposed to mean being in the image of God, which means—rejecting the animal nature we so closely resemble and embracing the divine image in each and every one of us. That means—we are all, even the bad ones among us—image bearers of God, not monsters or animals.

It is hard to see the image of God in the person who abuses and harasses you, however. I truly do not believe change was possible for my ex-husband. I wanted it to be possible. I wanted it more than anything. I also recognized that short of a miracle, short of God changing his heart, that was not going to happen.

It didn't change my praying for it. It didn't change my continuing to hold him accountable for what he did. He deserved to go to prison. He deserved to pay for the things he had done to people. While I did not wish any of his troubles on him, I also did not excuse what he had done to others.

And I did not excuse the unwitting part I played in enabling him for a time. While I recognize I was being manipulated into seeing only a particular version of him and didn't have all the information, it doesn't excuse that I continued to stay married to him and even defended him for a time. I take ownership of that.

I also take ownership of the reality that I saw and believed what I wanted to see and believe at the time. As pointed out early on, I knew I was compromising when I married him. He wasn't perfect. He wasn't everything I was looking for in a spouse.

I had simply given up by the time I was thirty-eight that finding that person to share my life with was even possible. So I compromised and married someone who I knew would be a challenge to live with. I knew his daughter had a lot of problems and that would be a challenge to cope with as well. I did not realize most of her problems were not solely the result of her drug-addicted, bi-polar mother, but that she was undergoing an even more devastating level of narcissistic abuse than I had been subjected to. But that's her story to tell, not mine. Regardless, I was arrogant in my own right, believing that I could handle whatever was thrown at me. That love was enough to overcome whatever challenges life would throw our way.

I soon discovered I was wrong. Just being committed was not enough. Just loving someone was not enough. I told my mother one time, "I knew it was going to be hard, but I had no idea it was going to be a living hell."

In many ways, part of what I needed to do in the process of forgiving him was forgiving myself for a lot of things. Forgiving myself for not paying attention to the red flags that I saw prior to us ever getting married. Forgiving myself for not seeing or being fully aware of the abuse that was going on with his daughter right in my own house and not putting a stop to it. Forgiving myself for not walking away sooner. Forgiving myself for not recognizing that his daughter, despite all of her anger and antics toward me that made me believe she truly hated me, needed to be rescued from her father. I'd written her off as a lost cause who was so messed up and co-dependent upon him that there was no possibility that I could do anything to have helped her. I'm still not sure given the circumstances I could have, but I didn't really honestly even try. I need to forgive myself for that.

I had to release not only the relationship, but I had to release my anger, my animosity, my grief, my guilt—not so much for his sake, but for my own. I needed to be free of that.

I refer to myself as a survivor now, rather than a victim.

And forgiveness is not a static thing. There will be moments where the anger bubbles up over the life and the future and the dream that were all taken from me, and I have to forgive all over again. It's a conscious and ongoing act of releasing it and handing it all over to God. It isn't that you just forgive and everything is forgotten.

The guilt as well somedays rears its head, and I have to figure out how to forgive myself all over again.

It's forgiving and releasing it—over and over and over again.

Seventy times seven.

Nineteen

Creation Song

*"Until one has loved an animal,
a part of one's soul remains unawakened."*

— Anatole France

IN DISNEY FILMS, ANIMALS take on the roles of friends and sometimes even family. In the original folktale of *Mulan*, she was said to have a "little brother." Disney turned that little brother into a cute little dog that she named (wait for it): "Little Brother." There was Mushu, the dragon, and Khan, the horse, as her companions. Or the mice in *Cinderella*. Jiminy Cricket as *Pinocchio's* friend and conscience. Animals provide friendship and comfort when humans fail to provide what is necessary.

God said that animals were not a suitable companion for Adam...but when God has clearly not seen fit to give you a human companion, and a dog is the only companion God's going to give you, you cling to it.

One of the primary elements in my healing process was my dog, George. He gets brief mentions in this story, but I never focus or spend much time on how he truly helped me through some of my most difficult days.

George literally became my child. I realized when I filed for divorce, all my hopes and dreams of ever having a family were over.

But I had my beloved dog. A dog who had an array of expressions and loved me so unconditionally that he was never far from my side. The dog who bonded with me, not my husband, because two weeks after we got him, my husband went to jail. The two were seemingly tied together in a strange way, as though God provided me with the emotional support animal I needed before I knew I needed it. I didn't even really want a dog based on my lifestyle and knowing I didn't have the time to let one out, walk them, train them. But Cavalier King Charles' are literally the most adaptable, calm, loving dogs you could ever hope for.

George gave me a reason for being. He gave me a reason to get up in the mornings when I just wanted to not face the world. He gave me a reason to keep on living and not just curl up and die. It may say sound strange, but whenever I would have thoughts about ending my own life to escape the chaos and the turmoil—I would think of George. How long would it take them to find me? How hungry would he be? How traumatizing would it be for him to be in a house with his dead owner?

I know it sounds awful and morbid, but he really and truly was what kept me going. He kept me alive simply by existing.

He eventually became not just a mere pet, but an integral part of my life. After I moved to Florida, he would come to work with me and was a constant presence in my life. He followed me wherever I went to the point I didn't even need a leash for him most of the time.

More people tended to know me as "George's mom" than by my name at the apartment complex I lived in for the first few years in Florida. At church, parishioners would frequently not bother asking me how I was doing, but would want to know how George was doing.

He passed away suddenly and tragically on my first day at a new church site. We were walking between the sanctuary and the office and I was pushing a cart with a computer on it. Behind me, George was following along like he typically did.

Then something caught his attention; he paused and began sniffing something just off the side of the sidewalk. I didn't get a good look at what it was, but I could see he was trying to eat it. He tried to eat everything. Rolling my eyes, I stopped pushing the cart and turned around to grab him by the harness and yank him away from whatever it was he was trying to consume.

Knowing I was likely going to deprive him of his new-found prize, he gulped whatever it was down.

His reaction was immediate and violent. He tried to throw whatever it was up to no avail. When that didn't work, he began crawling into the grass, and I immediately scooped him up in my arms realizing whatever he'd eaten was doing something terrible to him.

He went limp in my arms as I picked him up and rushed to the car. By the time I placed him on the passenger side seat, his eyes had glazed over, a small froth of foam ringed his lips, and he was no longer breathing. I screamed in gut-wrenching agony as I realized he was already dead, but I refused to accept it.

I jumped in the driver's side and sped to the nearest vet that was ten minutes away.

I didn't make it to the first stoplight before I could smell his bowels expelling.

He was dead. I knew it. But I numbly continued driving to the vet.

I'll never know what exactly it was he consumed that killed him so quickly. The vet thinks it had to have been something that was likely laced with fentanyl in order for it to act so fast. Bufo toads, rat poison, mushrooms—everything else would take at least fifteen to twenty minutes if not hours to kill him.

I was inconsolable. Beyond devastated.

I'd lost my child. I'd lost my constant companion who had seen me through every step of my divorce. During the divorce hearing, the judge had asked us why we wanted the dog.

My ex's response had been because he was worth a lot of money.

My response was that he was family. He was my baby.

Thankfully, I was awarded custody of the dog.

In a weird and awful way, it seemed fitting that I lost George when I did. He was sort of my final tie to my ex, and as I began to realize, those ties seemed to all be disappearing in unexpected ways.

But George in life, as much as in death, reminded me of our close connection to animals in the creation story, where God speaks animals into existence just before he speaks humanity into existence.

Or, as the case may be, sang us all into existence.

Genesis 1 is sometimes referred to as a Hebrew "creation hymn," reflecting the mystery, grandeur and beauty of the act of creation. In C.S. Lewis' *The Magician's Nephew*, (the precursor to *The Lion, the Witch and the Wardrobe*) there is the scene where Aslan sings creation into existence. Similarly, in J.R.R. Tolkein's *Silmarillian*, angelic beings perform a great musical symphony, prefiguring the creation of the material universe. Such literary scenes are drawn not only from the melodic, repetitive nature of the Genesis 1 account, but from its description of the act of creation that is born out of God speaking the universe into existence.

People get so caught up in the order and the arguments over amounts of time, evolution, etc., that they completely miss the point and the cosmic scope of the prose. I attempted to grab hold of the canorous quality and the sense that life bursts forth from the musical notes of wisdom's song.

The 'musica universalis' (universal music) is an ancient philosophical concept that the movement of the celestial bodies is a harmonic movement rooted in mathematics, a metaphysical premise whereby mathematical relationships express qualities or "tones" of energy which manifest in numbers, visual angles, shapes and sounds. Pythagoras proposed that the Sun, Moon and planets all emit their own unique hum (orbital resonance) based on their orbital revolution, and that the quality of life on Earth reflects the tenor of celestial sounds which are physically imperceptible to the human ear.

Those who know me undoubtedly see the irony in which I embrace the mathematical (the bane of my existence, typically) as being part of the heart and soul of the musical and artistic. But like everything in life, I don't have to necessarily fully understand it to appreciate it.

As I have been on my healing journey, it has been this sort of rhythmic connection to the creation and all life that has resonated deeply with me and been a part of my process. Of how all things truly are connected and tie together as the notes and chords within the symphony of life.

That the God of creation and life is still speaking and singing. That George may no longer be with me, but he will forever be part of the Creation Song that brought us all into existence.

I miss George every day and despite the love and affection I now have both from and for my new puppy, Gracie, I still miss the connection the two of us had. The way we just knew each other's habits and even moods.

But this God of creation who spoke us into existence will not let death and separation have the last word. This I know.

I know that if I have the capacity to love my dog like he was my own child, God loved George, too. God created George, after all, and I firmly believe that given God loves far more deeply and perfectly than I am able to, that he not only loves George, but like the rest of creation, he will be redeemed and restored one day.

Twenty
Renewal & Rebirth

"God uses broken things. It takes broken soil to produce a crop, broken clouds to give rain, broken grain to give bread, broken bread to give strength. It is the broken alabaster box that gives forth perfume. It is Peter, weeping bitterly, who returns to greater power than ever."

— Vance Havner

WHILE FAIRY TALES DON'T tend to cover themes of forgiveness, they do cover come-uppance. They frequently make sure we know that the villain in the story eventually got what was coming to them.

In my world, I never wished harm on my ex-husband despite everything he did. I simply wanted him to leave me alone and to not hurt other people anymore. While I had taken steps to ensure he could not hurt me anymore, there was nothing I could do about the latter. Events would unfold, however, that would take care of that.

When I stated that George was seemingly the last tie I had to my ex-husband, it's because four months earlier, I had received a text message from my former brother-in-law with whom I'd stayed in contact. We both had known and experienced the worst parts of his brother. We knew who and what he was, and neither one of us had ever been interested in sugar coating the realities.

The text message was simple. "Can I call you?"

I texted back, "Sure." I braced myself, figuring he was going to fill me in on some new crazy accusation, as it had only been a few months earlier that he'd reached out to tell me about how my ex had accused him of conspiring with me to steal his daughter's college fund. We'd shared a good laugh at the fact that the fund he was referring to we both knew he had drained a long time ago.

That was not what this phone call was about.

On September 15, 2022, my ex-husband had ended his life with a bullet to the chest in Nashville, Tennessee.

I'm not going to lie, I didn't really know how to feel about this initially. I was, of course, stunned and didn't really know what to say except, "Oh."

I felt a combination of grief, relief, and guilt (for feeling relieved)—needless to say, my feelings were complicated.

I knew he had been incapable of loving me, and that he in fact did not love me. His daughter was able to verify that he had flat out told her that he didn't love me, but he needed me so they would still have a place to live after he lost the house and that I could help shield him from the worst consequences of his actions given my role as a pastor in the community.

None of that changed the fact that despite knowing I'd compromised when I married him, I did still love him for whatever reason. I still cared about him, and I never ever would have wished death on him, even though many of my friends and family did. Most of them were not at all sorry he was dead, and in fact, even stated they felt bad for what I was going through, but they were not sad or sorry that he had killed himself.

I understood their feelings, and I cannot lie—I shared in their relief that he was no longer going to be able to hurt anyone anymore.

It was a surreal experience watching his memorial service online. It was strange to see how easily I'd been erased from his life as there was no mention of our marriage, no pictures that involved us, which was fine. I didn't expect I would be part of the service in any way. It just was strange. It was also strange to listen to his friends, almost none of whom I knew—he had pretty much burned through any friends he'd had when we were together, which was typical for a narcissist—talk about what a giving and wonderful person he was.

That made me mad at first. Then I realized that the reason I was mad was that was how I had once experienced him as well.

Until he changed. Or rather, until his mask dropped and his true self came out. It's not those people's fault that they hadn't known him long enough to have him turn his abusive behavior on them, and I guess I was jealous that they were able to still remember him that way.

I should have been grateful, not bitter, that they never had to endure that side of him.

His brother got up, however, and stated, "I'm so glad you experienced him in this way. Unfortunately, as his family, we knew a much darker side." Later, his brother would text me, "It's a pity that he treated his friends so generously and his family so poorly."

Funerals are difficult places to speak hard truths, but I was glad that his brother was able to at least offer up that. While his friends who had only known him for a short time were mourning and grieving, many others were a lot less upset by his death. Especially the women he had targeted and abused. And our friends who witnessed the abuse.

Some of my friends even went so far as to say they hoped he was rotting in hell.

Again, I did not wish that for him. At all. He had hurt a lot of people, and I don't want to diminish that. I believe as well that the primary reason he took his own life was because he was facing more legal problems due to his entanglements with what turned out to be the wrong woman.

That third woman I simply couldn't involve myself with was attempting to deal with the threats he was making. Apparently, he had slept with her and then discovered she had a boyfriend. He demanded she pay him fifteen-hundred dollars not to tell her boyfriend. She called his bluff and turned him in for felony extortion.

For three years he'd been pulling all of his typical delay tactics in the court room. Demanding a new judge, telling them he wasn't available for court dates because he was out of town, using his mother who was dying of stage four lung cancer as an excuse—until the judge finally told him no more delay tactics. His case was going to trial.

He was facing seven to fifteen years in prison for that, and in typical form for him, she had all the iron-clad evidence of voicemails, emails, and text messages. Additionally, he'd also recently once again been caught in a recording making threats to a landlord. I didn't get all the details. They didn't matter.

Now, I can't say for sure the only reason he chose to end his life was because he could not handle the prospect of spending several years in state prison after his brief four-month stint in federal prison. It is believed that part of why narcissists are narcissists is because deep down and at their core they suffer from a very poor self-image, that they do not have good self-esteem. The narcissism is a by-product of that self-loathing, where they overcompensate to make themselves more important than they are.

Thus, they are far more prone to depression and suicidal tendencies. Ten years earlier he had scored a sixty on the Global Assessment Functioning (GAF) scale.

The GAF is used to rate how serious a mental illness may be. It measures how much a person's symptoms affect their day-to-day life on a scale of 0 to 100. It's designed to help mental health providers understand how well the person can do everyday activities and function within normal society.

A sixty meant he had "moderate" symptoms and still functioned pretty normally, though experienced conflicts with others like co-workers, family and friends.

Now reading over his court-ordered assessment and the responses he gave to the therapist, I know he lied about his suicidal ideation and desires to harm himself, which probably is what resulted in a much higher score. In retrospect, he likely should have been fifty or below. (A fifty meant: suicidal ideation, severe obsessional rituals, impairment in social, occupational and school settings, such as being unable to keep a job for long or maintain relationships.) While we were married, he had frequently talked about killing himself. I eventually began to dismiss them as merely a manipulation tactic to keep me from leaving him. There was also that time he had been put on suicide watch while he was in prison just before I filed for divorce.

So I recognize that depression likely did play a role. The signs were all there. The threats were there, whether any of us took them seriously or not.

Yet, I still believe the driving force had more to do with trying to escape the consequences of his actions. Either way, given his propensity for threatening to kill himself, the news that he had finally done it should not have really shocked me, and I don't know that it fully did.

By September of 2022, we had been officially divorced for almost seven years—separated for nine. Yet I still had a security system in my home because I never knew if he might decide to show up on my doorstep and try to hurt me. As much as I had hoped that he had fully moved on, it had become clear he had not. In fact, he'd told his daughter that I had moved in order to stalk him. Which was an interesting trick of mine given I moved a year before he did. I guess those super-powers to predict the future went along with my ability to control the weather and flood his storage unit. I also know that narcissists project the things they are doing onto others and accuse them of what they are actually doing. So that didn't sit very well with me, either, knowing the possibility existed that he had moved to stalk me.

Every accusation tends to be a confession.

He also continued to accuse me of stealing from him, and claimed in a letter to his daughter that I still owed him thousands of dollars, but he just didn't think it was worth continuing to take me to court over it. And for the record, that letter was written in 2019, three years before he actually did the deed. He was simply trying to guilt his daughter and blame her for his death. He truly was despicable in that way.

There was indeed a sense of relief that came with the knowledge that I would no longer have to look over my shoulder. I would no longer have to constantly wonder if and when he was going to just show up and wreak havoc in my life.

I do not ever want to say that I think the world might actually be a better place without him in it, but if I'm being completely honest: I feel the world might actually be a better place without him in it.

As a pastor, I struggle with that statement. I struggle with that feeling. Yet the reality is no one else can be harmed by him, and that is a good thing.

But I also do not wish him to "rot in hell" as some of my friends and family might desire. What I do know is that whatever hell he was in was a hell of his own making. I honestly hope he has found some sort of peace that he was unable to find in this life.

While I understand he killed himself in an effort to avoid accountability, that he didn't want to face the consequences of his actions; I'm not sure it works that way. While I believe God is a merciful and loving God, I also believe God is a just God. Whatever he faces in the afterlife, I ultimately do turn it over to God to deal with, and I trust that God will do what is right.

I hope he is able to be transformed in death in ways he was never able to be changed in life. If there is anyone who is in desperate need of a transformed life, a rebirth, if you will, it was him.

As for me, I've known for years that I'll never be the same person I was prior to my marriage. None of us are the same a decade later regardless, but I know my experiences having been subjected to narcissistic abuse changed much of how I viewed the world going forward. I no longer question why women don't leave abusive relationships. It's dangerous and difficult to do so. I had the perfect storm of circumstances that allowed me to "easily" get away in comparison to a lot of women. Still, it was by no means easy.

I still have PTSD triggers; though they've gotten better with time. They don't entirely go away. I'm no longer bothered by the mailman, for instance. Still, I discovered recently that when someone goes off on me in a narcissistic rage rant, that's still triggering as all get out. It will cause me to become paralyzed and incapable of doing much besides collapsing in a puddle of tears. If you aren't familiar with how PTSD works, when you get triggered it transports you back to the same emotions and fears that you experienced back when the initial trauma happened. For example, when military veterans hear fireworks that sound like gun shots, they're transported back to whatever hellish fire-fight they were part of. Triggers can last moments, hours, days, or even years.

It's extremely hard to work in an environment where others don't comprehend or understand what your PTSD is like. When people want you to just "get over it" or move on from a triggering incident. That's not how that works. Lack of compassion in such cases can itself wind up being a traumatizing event, compounding the issue.

Still, I emerged from the ashes of the death of my relationship and was reborn a changed woman, but in many ways a better woman. I've become more keenly aware of abusive, and especially narcissistic, behavior. I've become an advocate for abused women and other marginalized groups.

I've determined I will hopefully never compromise again or ignore red flags when I see them. I realize this is easy to say when I have no prospects. That doesn't mean I won't be hurt. I'll still make mistakes and probably more bad choices—but once the red flags start popping up, I sincerely hope I recognize it's time to cut the relationship off. I hope I will listen to my friends when they see it and call it out.

And I hope for friends and family that will always call it out. I will listen. I may not agree, but I will always listen without anger, without animosity. I know such concern comes from a place of deep love and care.

I will likely still take chances on love—like my ill-fated attempts with the pilot.

I've made as much peace as I think I can with the fact that I will never have that which I had spent my life dreaming about. I'm too old now to have that family I so desperately wanted, and quite frankly, too tired to even contemplate what it would be like to try once you're over the age of fifty. I'm no Sarah, and I don't want to be.

I have hope that maybe someday I'll still find someone that is able to actually love me romantically, who will see my gifts and love me for them.

Yet that "tick...tick...tick" of the years continue to ricochet around in my head. Not for a family, but simply for the time that remains in my life to have the kind of relationship I've always wanted and dreamed about. That person who is your best friend and companion. That you share everything with. That laughs at all of life's little foibles with you. That you can be content just curling up and watching a movie with, or going out on the town dressed to the nines.

I grieve the thought of not having someone as I age to grow old with so we can take care of one another. I stress about my future, knowing I never had children. What will happen to me should I get Alzheimer's or some other debilitating, but not necessarily deadly, disease? Pastors live isolated lives.

So I worry.

The other struggle is I still haven't figured out what exactly I'm here to do, what I'm here to accomplish other than maybe it's something as simple as to tell my story so that others can find healing and hope.

Maybe when God told me, "I have other plans for you," that's part of what he was talking about. I don't know.

I don't really adhere to the belief that God causes us to be in harmful situations in order to teach us a lesson we can then help others through. I'm more of the belief that he takes those terrible situations and experiences and uses them for good.

No one knows the future—despite what my dear little psychic friend may claim. And while I will not allow my past to dictate my future, I have learned from it. I think the lesson I learned was not, "Don't love. Don't open your heart again."

That might be the safer way. But it's not my way.

I don't know where my "fairy tale" life is headed at this juncture. I certainly would not classify where I'm at a "happy ending." Mainly because I'm just entering my fifties and I really hope there's a lot more to my story than this, just hopefully with less heartache and betrayal.

I don't have illusions that my life will have the long-standing impacts other members of my family have had, who have managed to do things that literally affect and save lives all around the world. My father helped invent Advanced Trauma Life Support (ATLS) training that is now utilized worldwide to train emergency room doctors and nurses. (If you ever want to read more about how that came about, there's a book by Randy Styner called, *The Light of the Moon: Life, Death and the Birth of Advanced Trauma Life Support,* that recounts how a tragic plane crash outside Hebron, Nebraska that claimed the life of his mother led to his and my father developing this training program in the mid-seventies.) I also have a brother who has over sixty patents from his job at 3M working on dental adhesives. If you have a composite filling in your mouth, my brother was probably responsible for developing that.

I doubt whatever "plans" God has for me are quite that grand or important. After all, I've never really been trying to change the world beyond my little corner of it. I wanted the provincial life, after all.

Am I simply destined to be the mermaid who eventually becomes part of the sea? Or will there one day be that person who sees me and knows me in a way I've always desired?

As I said, no one knows the future.

However, I'm glad I was able to write this part of my story and put it out there for others to maybe learn from and find some solace in their own situations. To know they're not alone. To know there is a light at the end of the tunnel.

So much of this seems like another lifetime ago, and I suppose that's because it is. I was only married a short time—it was a blip on my otherwise single life. Yet those few years dramatically shaped and altered who I am today.

In this final painting, I specifically chose the imagery of a lotus flower/water lily. They're different flowers, but for these purposes, it doesn't really matter which it is. Both the water lily and the lotus are symbols of creation, new life, and resurrection. The lotus flower/water lily both have deeply ancient symbolic roots in Egyptian, Buddhist, and Hindu religious traditions. In Egyptian mythology, it was noted that the lotus/lily closed and submerged under water during the night but then re-emerged and opened in the morning. It thus became associated with both creation and re-birth.

In Hinduism, the lotus primarily represents beauty and non-attachment. The lotus/lily is rooted in the mud but floats on the water without becoming wet or muddy. This symbolizes how one should live in the world in order to gain release from rebirth: without attachment to one's surroundings.

The meaning in Buddhism is similar, as the lotus/lily is seen rising and blooming above the murk to achieve enlightenment. It also resembles the purifying of the spirit which is born into murkiness. Faithfulness is likewise represented as those who are working to rise above the muddy waters will need to be faithful followers.

Rising above the muck and mire.

That's what I've had to do. Not just rise above, but bloom and thrive despite the dark, gross, muddy circumstances I had to wade my way through to get here. This painting is thus about new life and new experiences, of moving on to something new. The next chapter of my life that has yet to be written. Not becoming too attached to places or things as they are temporary elements of life. Our world is an ever-changing world that requires at times deep faith to cope and manage the major changes life has in store for us. And a realization that faith is not easy, and human representatives more often than not can fail us in our times of need.

While this painting is about rising above the murkiness in life, growing through the mud and coming out beautiful and clean on the other side, it's also a reminder that the murkiness, the ick, the mud, is still there. We float on top of it, but it still exists.

In Christianity, it's symbolic to me of the "now and not yet." We are washed clean yet still live our lives in the midst of the murkiness. Cleansed—but not removed from the muck. Beautiful in the sight of God—but still mired in a world that groans for redemption.

This is ultimately the image and hope that I cling to with my faith: that image of the Kingdom of God. Where there will be no more pain, no more death, and no more tears.

"He will wipe away every tear from their eyes, and death shall be no more, neither shall there be mourning nor crying nor pain any more, for the former things have passed away." (Revelation 21:4)

We get glimpses of this world, glimpses of what awaits.

In the meantime, we forge forward. We get hurt. We heal. We forgive. We love.

Over and over.

There is nothing new under the sun.

I haven't let the trauma, the pain, the hurt, close me down to the point my heart no longer has the capacity to love. I hope this is a good thing, not a destructive thing.

Someday, I hope to love again. Someday, I hope to be loved in return.

Someday, I hope for my "happily ever after." I had hoped that when I finally wrote this book, that I would be able to end on that note. To let others know that there is life and love beyond the trauma.

There is definitely life. Love? That remains to be seen. Others find it. I simply haven't. But that's my story, not your story.

And both are still being told.

To be continued...

To contact Rebecca J. Craig for speaking engagements,
or to view or purchase her artwork,
please visit rebeccajcraig.com.

Many Voices. One Message.

quoir.com

Made in the USA
Columbia, SC
20 October 2024